D0597170

with

Coping

DISCRIMINATION AND PREJUDICE

Mary Bowman-Kruhm, Ed.D., and
Claudine Wirths, M.A., M.Ed.

The Rosen Publishing Group, Inc.
New York

Published in 1998, 2000 by The Rosen Publishing Group, Inc.
29 East 21st Street, New York, NY 10010

Copyright © 1998, 2000 by Mary Bowman-Kruhm and Claudine Wirths

Revised Edition 2000

Library of Congress Cataloging-in-Publication Data

Bowman-Kruhm, Mary.
Coping with discrimination and prejudice / Mary Bowman-Kruhm and Claudine Wirths.
Includes bibliographical references and index.
Summary: Examines the causes and effects of prejudice and discrimination and discusses how to confront and cope with them.
    ISBN: 0-8239-3299-0
    1. Prejudices in children—juvenile literature. 2. Discrimination—Juvenile literature. 3. Racism—Juvenile literature. [1. Discrimination. 2. Prejudices.] I. Wirths, Claudine G. II. Title.
BF723.P7B68 1998
303.3'85—dc21

                                                    98-21292
                                                         CIP
                                                          AC

Manufactured in the United States of America

About Mary Bowman-Kruhm, Ed.D.

Mary Bowman-Kruhm, Ed.D., is a writer and faculty associate at Johns Hopkins University School of Professional Studies in Business and Education. She is a contributing editor to *Children's Book Insider* newsletter. Bowman-Kruhm has authored, or coauthored with Claudine G. Wirths, twenty-five books. *I Hate School: How to Hang In & When to Drop Out* (Harper & Row, 1987) was named by the American Library Association on its lists Best Books for Young Adults—1986 and Recommended Books for Reluctant Young Adult Readers—1987, and by the National Council of Teachers of English in Books for You (recommended under Self-Help and Easy Reading categories).

Other books for teens and young adults include *Where's My Other Sock? How to Get Organized & Drive Your Parents & Teachers Crazy* (Harper, 1989), *I Need a Job* (J. Weston Walch, 1988), *Are You My Type? Or Why Aren't You More Like Me?* (Consulting Psychologists Press, 1992), *How to Get Up When Schoolwork Gets You Down* (David C. Cook, 1993), *I Need to Get Organized* (Walch, 1993), *Word Power, Your Circle of Friends,* and *Your New School* in the Time to Be a Teen series for Henry Holt/21st Century Books (1993), *Choosing Is Confusing: How to Make Good Choices, Not Bad Guesses* (CPP/Davies-Black Publishing, 1994), *Upgrade: The High Tech Road to School Success* (CPP/Davies-Black Publishing, 1995), *I Need to Get Along with Different Types of People* (Walch, 1995), and *Coping with Confrontations and Encounters with the Police* (Rosen, 1997). *Money: Save It, Manage It, Spend It* (Enslow) and *Careers in Child Care* (Rosen) are in press.

For younger children, she has authored nine beginning readers in the Rosen series, A Day in the Life of. A picture book, *Busy Toes* (Charlesbridge/Whispering Coyote, 1998), was written with Claudine Wirths and Wendie Old under the pen name C. W. Bowie.

In addition, Bowman-Kruhm is the author of numerous articles and stories in professional journals and magazines as diverse as *VOYA, The Learning Disabilities Association Advocate,* and *Vegetarian Times.*

About Claudine Wirths

Claudine G. Wirths, M.A., M.Ed., is a full-time writer and consultant. She has authored over twenty books with Dr. Mary Bowman-Kruhm.

As a research social psychologist, Ms. Wirths has also authored nine monographs and numerous articles. Professional positions include adjunct faculty member at Frederick (Maryland) Community College, coordinator of a program for adolescents with learning disabilities, head teacher of a school for students identified as retarded, and elementary science teacher at a private school.

Acknowledgments from the Authors

Many thanks are due colleagues and friends who helped us:

Dorothy Carpenter, Montgomery County (Maryland) Public Schools; Delores B. Cole, tenant counselor, low-income housing; Glenda Cole-Bobo, Montgomery County Public Schools; Sam Fulwood, III, correspondent, *Los Angeles Times*; Rosemary Garr, Montgomery County Public Schools; the Reverend Columba Gilliss; Joan Lumley, Montgomery County Public Schools; Karen L. Moore; Darryl Norwood, Montgomery County Public Schools/court liaison; Dion and Jenny Johnson; and Richard Sakurai.

Acknowledgements from Mary Bowman-Kruhm

Thanks also to my husband, Carl Kruhm, and children, Jean Eargle, Bonnie Redmond, and Hope McGonigle, and to Claudine, Ted, David, and Bill Wirths, all of whom provided ideas, memories, perceptions, and information.

Contents

Introduction:
Discrimination Lives, but Does It Thrive?

As I worked on the revision of this book, the question in my mind was, "Is discrimination as strong a force in our world, and especially in the United States, as it was five years ago when Claudine Wirths and I wrote the first edition?"

To answer this question, I gathered statistics, observed, read, and talked to many people, including writer and correspondent for the *Los Angeles Times* Sam Fulwood III.

What did I find out? I am still shocked by accounts of acts of discrimination. Why, I ask myself, did professional baseball player John Rocker choose to offend so many people, including his own teammates, with his hostile words about blacks, gays, immigrants, and anyone not like him? Why are places of worship still burned and defaced? Why isn't there peace in parts of the world where people have been fighting for hundreds of years?

On the other hand, when I asked Sam Fulwood III if he feels race matters have improved, he replied, "Absolutely!" My own research into areas like gender, religion, and disability confirms a sense of improvement or, at least, the desire to improve.

I believe that this improvement is due primarily to young people. I watch young people of all races and ethnic groups relating to each other more easily now than ever before. I have read many Web pages written by young people all over the world who want to stop acts of discrimination. My grandson is more concerned about the fun he and his best friend share than the fact that his friend's skin is a different color than his own. I know he is not alone.

I have revised this book with a sense of hope. Unfortunately, discrimination still exists, but it does not seem to be thriving.

Issues of discrimination and prejudice are complex. Through dialogue and by translating thought into action, young people like you can send discrimination into retreat.

Prejudices:
Everyone Has 'Em

You and your friend get in line at a fast-food restaurant. A very heavy woman is in front of you. Your friend chuckles. "That woman just ordered a double burger, shake, and large fries! Just what she needs!" You nod and laugh, too.

You and your friend have just made fun of someone based on your prejudices about overweight people. You prejudged her because of her looks. You did not know anything about her. Prejudging someone based on little or no information (or on the wrong information) and according only to one's own background, values, biases, and opinions is called prejudice. (See where the word prejudice comes from?—*Pre* means "before" and *judge* means "decide.")

We All Have Prejudices

As Brad begins to back his car out of a parking spot, a car eases in front of him. The driver is an elderly woman with glasses. Brad mutters to himself, "Great! I'm already late and now some old lady who is driving way under the speed limit will hold me up even more. She shouldn't even be on the road."

Brad is prejudiced against older drivers. Having prejudices is common. We each have them. It is what we do with those thoughts and beliefs and why we have them that is important.

Where Do Our Prejudices Come From?

Most prejudices are learned. We tend to value what those close to us—our parents, friends, and teachers—value. Our prejudices are based on those values. Some values we develop from our life experiences. We also get messages from song lyrics, books, television, and movies.

Our prejudices come from all these places and more. In most cases, trying to figure out exactly where our prejudices come from is not possible. Brad probably could not pinpoint what made him feel prejudice toward older drivers in the first place.

Broad Statements

Sometimes we close our minds to new information. Changing how we feel about something can be hard. Grouping all people into types and making broad, sweeping statements about them is a lot easier than looking at each person as an individual. It's one way we give our world order. These groupings can range from minor ("Rock stars aren't real musicians; they just use fancy equipment") to cruel ("All blond females are ditzy") to the hurtful ("White males should rule the world").

Look at the previous examples. In them the speaker feels:

➥ Rock musicians are not talented. The speaker doesn't take into consideration that musical talent

4

has nothing to do with the type of music that a person plays.

➾ Blond females are scatterbrained. But the color of someone's hair has nothing to do with a person's intelligence.

➾ White males are most fit for positions of power. We bet the speaker has not thought about the fact that people from all races and genders can be leaders.

Broad statements of prejudice are seldom true, since they cover such vast numbers of people in the groups to which they are referring.

Stereotypes

Like the statements above, many of our prejudices are based on thinking that everyone in a group shares the same traits. Thinking this way is called stereotyping.

We are all exposed to stereotypes. Movies and television use stereotypes to quickly tell viewers about people in the show. There is the woman with long flowing hair, high heels, and a tight skirt (sexy, but weak), the sidekick (goofy, but sweet and loyal), and the lead male who's there to see justice is done and who will get the woman, even in the face of awful dangers (tough, handsome, and heroic). As soon as you see these stereotypes, you think you know something about the characters. The writer relies on these assumptions to tell his or her story.

But when you carry those stereotypes over into real life, you are likely to make some big mistakes. Assumptions based on stereotypes often result in your making unfair judgements about the people around you. Stereotyping does not work because people are much more complex than the narrow definition that the stereotype covers.

The Difference Between Traits and Stereotypes

Groups do have traits in common. Traits are features people have inherited or been taught that tend to make them look or act a certain way. Most Hispanics have brown eyes. Many Irish have red hair.

Note that we said traits tend to make people look a certain way. Not all Hispanics have brown eyes. Many Irish do not have red hair.

When we stereotype, we believe everyone in a group has the same traits. This is not true. Though there may be some similarities between people of that group, not everyone exhibits them. It is always best to get to know people on an individual basis.

. . . I'm still getting a lot of responses from teens who are upset with the grandmother who wrote saying that today's teens are lazy, self-centered, stupid rebels who only watch television, drink alcohol, do drugs, and have sex.

—From the column "TwEEN 12 & 20" by
Robert Wallace, Ed.D.,
in the *Frederick* (MD) *Post*,
June 6, 1997.

Because of her own prejudices, the grandmother who wrote Dr. Wallace used a stereotype of young adults to form a biased and inflammatory opinion.

You may notice someone being prejudiced only when you do not agree with them or when you are the one who is hurt. But have you ever laughed at a joke (or maybe even told one) that involved negative remarks about another person's sex, race, or religion? Then you too have stereotyped people.

Think about a prejudice you have. Try to think why you adhere to that way of thinking.

Changing Your Mind Can Be Healthy

We will not tell you that certain prejudices are either right or wrong. We do, however, hope you are willing to examine your beliefs, to think about them, and perhaps to change them if you find they are built on false or oversimplified information.

Teen years are a time of change. It's a time when many people question the values they have been taught in an effort to develop their independence. In this book we hope to help you rethink your feelings and make healthy changes in your prejudices, if you want to and/or think you should.

One of the things that has helped me all my life I got from my rector when I was in high school. He said that I'd always be scarred (I've come to think of it as deformed) by the prejudices I'd already learned, but that I could be aware of that and try not to act on them.

7

Later I've come to think of myself as a recovering—not recovered!—racist.
> —The Rev. Columba Gilliss,
> Episcopal priest

What We'll Talk About in This Book

The goal of this book is to help you think about prejudice and discrimination and how negative acts, whether minor or major, affect you and others.

To help you, we will:

⇒ Talk about how negative acts that grow out of your prejudices are hurtful;

⇒ Talk about how you can cope with acts directed against you, whether these acts are loud and open or quiet and subtle;

⇒ Consider ways that you, by your words and actions, encourage people to feel prejudice and act on those prejudices.

What Is Discrimination?

You are in the dentist's chair, waiting for a new dentist, Dr. Lee Jones, to check your teeth. A woman dressed in white walks into the room. "Are you the hygienist?" you ask. "No," she says, "I'm the dentist."

Did you act on an assumption about what you think a dentist should look like? Are you prejudiced against female dentists?

Discrimination

Let's see if we can make sense of the word "discrimination." When we discriminate, we assess someone's traits and make a decision based on what we know and see.

We all learn to discriminate. Babies do not discriminate at first. When a newborn is crying, almost any pair of arms that rock and cuddle will comfort it. A baby does not make a distinction between arms that are old, young, male, female, beige, pink, brown, or black. But, by the time a baby grows to be a teen, he or she has a vast store of experiences and teachings, attitudes, feelings, and prejudices as a basis for all kinds of discrimination.

Acts of Discrimination Are Not Always Bad

People often use their store of experiences, teachings,

9

attitudes, feelings, and prejudices to help them discriminate in a positive way. We make thoughtful choices that keep us out of trouble. We keep ourselves safe by not driving with someone who is drinking. We avoid people who are acting in a menacing manner. These, and other instances, are, in truth, acts of discrimination, but we tend to think of them as choices, or distinctions, that we make. We see them as positive because they enrich our lives or keep us safe.

Most of us think of acts of discrimination in a negative way; negative feelings based on prejudices. In this book, when we use the words "discriminate" and "discrimination" we will focus on negative choices, because that is the way we most often use and understand those words.

Acts of Discrimination

Other people may ultimately be involved, but acts of discrimination start with one person. One person always has to take the first step. One man or woman has a negative feeling about someone and then says, "Ignore him," or "We don't want to include her," or "Let's get rid of him."

"Tawney," said the assistant principal, "I'm surprised that you would be so unkind. You never seemed to me to be that kind of person."

"I'm really not," said Tawney. "I guess I got carried away. Alicia said she didn't like Rocky and the rest of us just went along with her."

Discrimination Happens

We have all felt the sting of acts of discrimination. And we have also stung others. We may have ignored someone or joined in a joke that made some group look bad. Even if we did not mean to, we have slighted someone or said something that hurt someone's feelings.

We may not have realized what we did. If we did know, we may have questioned our intentions later. We may have told the person we did not mean what we said or did. Maybe we even said we were sorry.

We may truly feel we really are not "that kind of person." Maybe we are not. On the other hand, people seldom behave in random ways. What someone says or does is often one of many similar acts. Added together, these acts form a pattern of behavior.

> *Dillon loved to tell jokes. He had a favorite one that was very racist and he told it often. When no one else was around, Beth said to him quietly, "Dillon, that joke really bothers me. It's racist and I don't think it's even funny."*
>
> *Word soon got back to Beth that not only was Dillon still telling the joke, but he was also telling people about Beth's complaint to him.*

Levels of Discrimination

Think of acts of discrimination as stairs with three steps. Let's say a family of a different race or ethnic group moves into a nearby house. Without meeting them, the neighbors are not happy with the newcomers. How far up the stairs will they move?

11

☞ Low-Level Discrimination is the first step: No one visits or offers to show the newcomers around the neighborhood.

☞ Mid-Level Discrimination is the second step on the stairs: People openly ignore attempts by the new family to be friendly. They turn their backs when they see members of the family in the local stores. They do not allow their children to play with the newcomers' children.

☞ High-Level Discrimination is at the highest step of the stairs: Neighbors commit acts that either endanger the new family or make them feel endangered, such as sending threatening letters to warn the new neighbors that if they don't move, they will be sorry.

Low-Level Acts of Discrimination

In low-level acts of discrimination, behavior is subtle. The discriminator avoids or ignores a person or group. An onlooker or the person being discriminated against cannot know for sure that negative feelings are involved.

Someone who is discriminating against some person or some group at this level:

☞ Does not sit at the person's cafeteria table at lunch but will quietly remain seated if the person sits at his or her table.

☞ Goes out of the way to avoid social contact but acts polite if forced to be on the same team.

12

↝ Makes a face or rolls eyes when the person is praised.

↝ Tells jokes that poke fun at groups of people or uses names that are negative but, if called on such acts, says it's no big deal.

↝ Seems (and may in fact be) unaware that he or she is committing an act of discrimination.

This type of discrimination is probably the most common. We may feel such acts are OK—after all, everyone we are close to feels the same way. Or we may think telling a joke about an ethnic or racial group is harmless fun, not discrimination, so long as a member of that group does not hear us. But this is not the case.

Here is an example of a low-level act of discrimination:

> *Wendie worked with a German woman named Greta. To practice the language she had learned in high school and to be friendly, Wendie sometimes spoke German with Greta. One day Greta's sister visited. Greta spoke English when she introduced her to Wendie, but then laughed and said to her sister in German, "She thinks she can speak German!" Wendie understood what was said—but was so hurt she could not think of the right German words to reply.*

Mid-Level Acts of Discrimination

In mid-level acts of discrimination, behavior is more open and obvious but discrimination is still not always clear-cut. At this level, the discriminator, by speech or action, actively rejects a person or group. If asked, however, the person may give a good reason that has little or nothing to do with discrimination. Others suspect an act of discrimination and are pretty sure they know the feelings of the person doing the discriminating.

Someone who discriminates on this level:

➥ Makes sure that someone he or she is prejudiced against does not get in his or her club.

➥ Makes no effort to be polite about the group to which this person belongs.

➥ Based on his or her preconceived ideas, urges the boss not to hire a member of this group.

➥ Talks badly about this person or group and uses name-calling that is offensive.

➥ Makes little or no attempt to hide his or her prejudice.

Roseanne told the landlord that she and her friend Perry loved the small apartment and could pay the security deposit right now. The landlord looked at the couple. "So you two don't have the same last name?"

"No," Perry said, "We're not married yet."

"Well, I'll get back to you tomorrow," the landlord said. He mumbled to himself, "People oughta be married if they live together."

Roseanne didn't hear from the landlord for several days. She was not surprised when she called him and he told her he had rented to someone else. She saw what had happened as a clear act of discrimination against two unmarried people living together.

High-Level Acts of Discrimination

In high-level acts of discrimination, the discriminator actively works to hurt or to destroy a person or group. Behavior at this level is obvious to everyone.

Someone who is discriminating at this level of the discrimination stairs:

- ☞ Makes sure that the person fails to get a promotion at work.

- ☞ Commits acts that are rude, crude, or lewd to embarrass, threaten, or hurt the person.

- ☞ Attempts to prevent certain people from moving into his or her neighborhood.

- ☞ Gangs up on a player to cause injuries that keep the person from playing.

- ☞ Tells false stories about another person.

- ☞ Threatens a person's life.

- ☞ Joins a group that commits hate crimes.

High-level acts of discrimination leave no doubt in anyone's mind about the feelings involved. The police chief who orders officers to routinely stop and do drug searches of all black males driving expensive cars with out-of-state tags is taking a high-level action. This action leaves no one in doubt about the chief's prejudices.

Someone may also commit an awful act but do it anonymously, without letting others know who did it. Slashing tires or burning a place of worship are examples of this level of discrimination and are called hate crimes.

Definition of a Hate Crime

A hate crime is defined under specific penal code sections as an act or an attempted act by any person against the person or property of another individual or group which in any way constitutes an expression of hostility toward the victim because of his or her race, religion, sexual orientation, national origin, disability, gender or ethnicity. (Elements of crime statutes and protected classifications vary from state to state.) This includes but is not limited to, threatening phone calls, hate mail, physical assaults, vandalism, cross burnings, destruction of religious symbols, and fire bombings.

—From the Web site of the Anti-Defamation League, "Responding to Hate-Motivated Behaviors in Schools"

Moving Up the Stairs

There may only be a few steps up from a low-level act to a mid-level act and from a mid-level to a high-level. A cartoon that pokes fun at another race may be passed to a friend and then torn up; that is a subtle, low-level act of discrimination. If that same cartoon is posted on a bulletin board, it is a mid-level act. If a dead rat is wrapped in the cartoon and put in the locker of someone of that race at school or work, that is a high-level act.

Small acts of discrimination may not seem like a big deal. But no one knows for sure where they will lead. The eyes rolled to show dislike might be noted by those who then feel it is okay to carry out a high-level act of discrimination. The instructions on the Internet on how to make a bomb are not in themselves a high-level act—until someone uses the directions to make a bomb that kills someone.

"Why'd She Do That?"

Acts of discrimination are hard to label. We must know what lies behind the speech or actions of the discriminator.

We often cannot be sure an act of discrimination is intended, even if we are the discriminator. After all, we are not always honest with ourselves about why we act as we do. Making judgements about how someone else has acted, especially in low-level and mid-level acts of discrimination, is even harder.

There are vast numbers of possible reasons why people act in ways that might be, or might be interpreted as, acts of discrimination.

Tricia asked Ken to go to her office party. As Tricia introduced him to other guests, Ken—a tall, handsome man—realized that she had invited him primarily to show him off and impress people. She didn't seem to care about him as a person at all. He felt used.

On the way home, he told Tricia how he felt.

"Yes, I did invite you to show you off," responded

Tricia, bluntly. "So what? Men have done that to women for years!"

In the next chapter, we will look at how a different point of view toward an act can muddy the complex problem of discrimination even more.

To Think About

☞ A friend invites you to a party. "I've invited everyone we know except that new guy Michael. I think he's kind of strange." Michael is in your math class and you do not think he is strange at all. Would you tell your friend how you feel? Would you consider Michael's absence as not a big deal? Would you skip the party yourself? What would you do?

From My Point of View ...

Whether you are president of a million-dollar business or a junior in high school, you look at things from your own very personal P.O.V. (point of view).

Long before you speak or act you have been storing up both information and prejudices in your mind. You may not even be aware you are storing these things, but you are filing them in your brain every waking minute of every day.

You use this mix of information, prejudices, attitudes, and values to form your personal view of any situation. Your evaluation and understanding of a situation, such as an act of discrimination, is based in large part on your personal point of view.

Jean joined a group of friends just as Mike began to tell a joke.

"The infant scale was out for repairs, so the nurse asked this blonde woman to use the adult scale. She'd figure the baby's weight by weighing the woman and baby together on the adult scale, then weighing the mother alone and subtracting the second amount from the first. 'It won't work,' the blonde said. 'I'm not the mother, I'm the aunt.'

Everyone laughed, except Jean. She scrunched up her nose.

"I don't think that's funny, Mike. Blondes aren't always dumb. I'm blonde and I'm not dumb," she said. "Awww," shrugged Mike. "It's just a joke."

Viewpoint Is Everything

Like Jean and Mike, in almost every action we take, including acts of discrimination, our individual viewpoints differ. As we noted when we talked about the steps, or levels, of discriminatory acts, an action that one person may not consider discrimination at all or at most, a minor act of discrimination, may seem like a high-level act that is very hurtful to someone else.

Erin stood at the desk in the bank lobby. Her purse flopped open on the table as she worked to add and subtract numbers. When a figure walked over to the desk, Erin realized she was taking up most of the space on the desktop. She pulled her purse closer and snapped it shut.

Erin heard a voice whisper a biting curse. A young black man uttered a few more quiet curses at her. In the crowded bank she felt alone and afraid. She pushed her checkbook into her purse and left.

While Erin perceived herself as being courteous and making room for the newcomer, the young man read her actions as making a statement that young black men cannot be trusted next to an open purse.

Acts in which different viewpoints clash happen every day. We are going to talk about one, because it shows so well the problems we face in trying to understand discrimination and prejudice and how point of view affects the interpretation of possible acts of discrimination. The place where it happened doesn't matter. It could have been your hometown or anywhere across the United States.

Let us look at this one incident and see how people acted, based on the way each person saw the situation and the interpretation each person made of it.

Setting the Stage: A Halloween Party

A small history museum held an adult Halloween party. The directors asked guests to dress in costumes that represented a favorite poem from a Mother Goose book of 1918. The party was not segregated, but only whites attended. One guest did a lot of research to get her costume just right. Based on her costume and the poem she recited, the museum sponsor gave her first prize. This does not sound like a big deal, right? So why did this person's actions get into one of the country's biggest newspapers, hundreds of miles away? Here is the short report that traveled far:

Most guests laughed during a Halloween party at a museum when a woman in blackface acted out an old nursery rhyme using a racial epithet and won first place for her costume.
        —Washington Post, November 10, 1996

Because of who you are, you no doubt already have an opinion about what happened. You, in other words, have your own views about a woman who dresses in blackface and recites a poem with racial slurs. We said we weren't

21

going to try to change your views, but we do want you to think about them. What do you think about this situation?

Can We Agree This Was an Act of Discrimination?

Remember our discussion of discrimination? We said an act of discrimination happens when a person acts in a negative way toward another person or persons. The person acts this way because of prejudices.

We hope you can agree with us that, based on this definition, this incident is an example of an act of discrimination. Here is our reasoning:

- African Americans believe that blackface comedy was, and is, degrading.

- By wearing blackface and reciting a poem that used racial slurs, the woman, knowingly or not, showed disrespect for African Americans.

- The women acted this way without regard for the negative impact it might make on others.

But Wait, There's More . . .

Local newspapers gave a fuller picture of what happened.

With her face painted black, one guest based her costume on an 1869 nursery rhyme about ten boys who, one by one, choke to death, burn up, get chopped in half, or otherwise are eliminated. In the end, none of them is left.

The rhyme, which guests said was read aloud at least

once during the dinner party, begins: "Ten little nigger boys went out to dine / One choked his little self and then there were nine . . . "
—*Duluth News-Tribune*, November 8, 1996

Upset? Or a Setup?

We've already told you the woman won first prize. What do you suppose was the reaction of the museum staff later? Did the staff defend the action they took in giving the woman first prize? Again, here is an excerpt from a follow-up article:

"[Her costume] certainly was the most unique. Everyone praised her for the lengths she went to," [the museum director] said. "Our guests all seemed to have fun. Everyone was laughing and having a good time. I am distressed to know that someone left unhappy. This is the craziest thing. Imagine, someone being upset by a Mother Goose nursery rhyme."
—*St. Paul Pioneer Press*, November 9, 1996

What about the viewpoints of those in the audience? Here is how follow-up newspaper accounts described the actions of the guests (remember, they were all white) who were there:

↝ One guest "was shocked and notified the NAACP."
—*Washington Post*, November 10, 1996

↝ A woman who attended with her husband said, when interviewed, "I was appalled. I was hyperventilating, I was so shocked and ashamed . . . I was just livid.

23

I couldn't even talk. I hope to heavens we weren't the only couple offended by this."
—*Duluth News-Tribune,* November 8, 1996

☞ The museum reported "they didn't receive any complaints about the woman's costume."
—*Duluth News-Tribune,* November 8, 1996

Lots of people attended the party, which means there were lots of different views about what happened. Based on your point of view, what would your actions have been if you were there?

Reactions to the Incident

What were the actions of people after news of the incident became known? Let's look at how their viewpoints each gave a different spin to the meaning of the word *taste.*

☞ The National Association for the Advancement of Colored People (NAACP) replied, "We can't file a lawsuit. It isn't against the law to do something in poor taste."
—*Washington Post,* November 10, 1996

☞ The museum staff pointed out that history can't be changed. "It was very tasteful, very well done, and extremely inventive," [the museum director] said. "This party was supposed to be happening in 1918. And it would have been very appropriate for that time period to have someone dress up in blackface."
—*Duluth News-Tribune,* November 8, 1996

Dealing with Ugly History

Museum directors, as well as history teachers and historians, give a lot of thought to what is called "ugly history," those parts of history that happened but are not pretty or pleasant to revisit. Soon, museum directors from all over the United States were asked for their own views of what happened and were asked to suggest some better way to have dealt with the incident. Here are some of them:

> ᵔ Missouri Historical Society president Bob Archibald, who has headed several national museum organizations, said he would have asked the woman to go home and change. "Museums should never shy away from controversial issues," Archibald added. "But to tackle them at a Halloween party probably isn't the best thing."
> —*Duluth News-Tribune*, November 9, 1996

> ᵔ "We need to show our history, warts and all. We need to discuss it and bring it out and learn from it, hopefully so we don't repeat past mistakes," said Dick Welch, a professional historian for more than twenty years who now heads Lake Superior Museum of Transportation [Duluth, Wisconsin]. "But we have to do that in an educational way," he said.
> —*Duluth News-Tribune*, November 9, 1996

> ᵔ "If her intentions were to send a message that old fairy tales can be violent and demeaning,

then I applaud her for being gutsy," said Christy Matthews, director of African American programs at Colonial Williamsburg, Virginia. "But I question the context in which she brought it up. This nursery rhyme is really about the destruction of black children and how we all should think it's humorous."

☞ "To present the rhyme at a party emphasizes the humor," Matthews went on to say. "Better to have focused discussion on the more important issue of offensive and violent nursery rhymes."
—*Duluth News-Tribune,* November 9, 1996

In the city where the incident took place, the newly formed Human Rights Commission met to discuss what had happened. "We were formed to educate, educate, educate. This is an opportunity for us," a member said. Several workshops and meetings were held to discuss racism.

The spokesperson for the Human Rights Commission asked a question that was no doubt on the minds of many people "This is the challenge we face—how do you put different histories into an appropriate context for today?" He might also have asked how best to bring together the different views everyone has about such an incident.

We may not always know when we are saying or doing something that hurts others. Very often people say and do things that to some seem to be acts of discrimination when, in fact, they simply don't realize the hurt or harm they may cause. The woman who wore blackface may, for example, not have suspected the pain she would inflict on many blacks. We cannot know for sure what prompted her actions. We know only that quotes from the museum director noted that the guest was "not offensive. She was not intending to offend anyone" and she was "distressed" by the publicity.

Empathy: How to Deal with People Not Like Ourselves

Because we so often are not aware how others feel, the saying, "We cannot understand people until we walk in their shoes," has become widely used. In fact, this saying has been used so much that it has become hackneyed and trite.

The saying means that we must have the same experiences as other people if we hope to understand them. But, is that possible? No. If you are male, you can never truly understand how it feels to be female. Understanding what it means to be Hispanic, Asian, or African American, unless you are a member of that culture, is impossible. If you live in the inner city, the world of people who get up early to care for farm animals is one you know only from television.

But, this doesn't mean we should throw up our hands and decide that our point of view, since it is the only one we know, is the only one that counts.

"I think it's impossible to walk in someone else's shoes," says Sam Fulwood III, "but we can empathize with others." When we empathize, we do a lot of things. We try to identify with those not like us. We also try to understand them and be sensitive to their feelings.

Trying to empathize with others, no matter who they are, helps broaden our personal viewpoint. Opening our minds to the problems, lifestyle, or experiences lived by someone else can widen the range of what we see and how we interpret what we see.

When we empathize with others, we gain understanding as to why people act and think as they do. That wider view gives us lots of options about how we react to them. It also helps us cope with discrimination when and if we face it ourselves.

Where We've Been, Where We're Going

So far in this book we have talked about how prejudices can lead to acts of discrimination. We have also said that acts of discrimination are like stair steps. Viewing discrimination as steps from lesser acts to those more serious helps us better understand how complex issues and actions revolving around prejudice and discrimination are. In this chapter we saw that few acts of discrimination are clear-cut and that each of us has our own view. We also talked about how a broader understanding can help us avoid many acts of discrimination.

Gender Bias

Our struggle today is not to have a female Einstein get appointed as an assistant professor. It is for a woman schlemiel to get as quickly promoted as a male schlemiel.
—Bella Abzug, former New York congresswoman
(as quoted in *Treasury of Women's Quotations*)

Male versus Female

In the United States, as in many countries of the world, the roles of men and women are changing as women gain rights long denied to them. Some people feel such changes will destroy the traditional family structure. Many others feel these changes are good. Still others accept the changes but are upset by the confusion they bring. They believe that neither men nor women are now sure about their roles in life. And some people think changes are not happening fast enough.

One thing is certain, no matter what your point of view: Women in many countries are more equal to men in most aspects of life, from school to marriage to work, than they have been in the past. They are still, however, not treated as equal to men in many other areas of life.

Power Play

Since recorded history, men have held power. They have

set and enforced rules for gender behavior in the western world and many other parts of the world as well. For example, in the mid-1800s, women in most states could not vote, own property, or go to college. They were barred from most jobs. Women did not even gain the right to vote until 1920, although they had been agitating for it for over seventy years.

"The trouble for [women] all along has been the knowledge on the part of the politicians that we would vote intelligently. If the men who run the machines had thought that women could be handled by party leaders, we would have had our rights long ago."
—Interview with Susan B. Anthony,
Rochester Democrat and Chronicle, June 23, 1894,
as reported in The Elizabeth Cady Stanton &
Susan B. Anthony Papers Project Online,
http://ecssba.rutgers.edu

What about Today?

Today men still hold the power. Sixty-two percent of adults are women, yet women are at a disadvantage in:

- ➮ Holding positions of power. They comprise only 9 percent of the United States Senate, 12.9 percent of the House of Representatives, 13 percent of federal judges, and 9 percent of state judges.

- ➮ Earning power. Women make only about seventy-three cents to every dollar a man earns.

There seems to be some progress, however.

"I have worked for two great companies—Xerox and Bell Atlantic—and have never felt the discrimination you all have been discussing," a woman told the Webgrrls discussion group on pay inequity. "Maybe it's that I am young, and these things are a sign that the old boys are dying off."
—Sabra Chartrand, "Wage Report Sparks Online Duels Between Sexes," *New York Times,* November 9, 1997

Times, They Are a-Changin'

Gender roles began to change as women gained access to voting rights, birth control, medical treatment, and education. Many women now work during their children's early years. Most job opportunities are now open to women.

Nevertheless, both women and men struggle against the stereotyping that persists in the minds of many.

Boys Will Be Boys

When a baby goes home from the hospital, the boy will most likely be wrapped in a blue blanket and the girl's blanket will be pink. By the time a child reaches school age, he or she has been given thousands of subtle messages about what differentiates boys and girls from each other. Most of them, like "trucks are for boys and dolls are for girls," are societal, not biological.

M Is for Males—and Math

From the early grades on, boys and girls aren't treated equally in school either. Math and science are seen as male-dominated areas of study. Many teachers teach with this bias in mind. Research shows that teachers tend to call on males more often, give them more time to answer, and give them more praise for what they say. Many teachers also encourage boys to be aggressive and discourage girls from speaking out.

Some people think that these differences in gender abilities are biological. Others think the differences are taught by adults, peers, and society, not made by nature. Still others consider the situation a combination of both.

Sexual Harassment and Abuse: Always Unacceptable

With the changing roles of men and women, the problem of sexual harassment has increased. By middle school, most boys learn that actions such as making lewd comments or grabbing a girl's body are wrong. Such acts are now more likely to be called sexual harassment than flirting or teasing, as they were in the past.

Whether you are male or female, know that sexual harassment and abuse are forms of discrimination. Here are some suggestions to help you if you are sexually harassed:

⇝ Some people choose to ignore the harassment, but others believe that it is better and more effective to ask the person to stop immediately. Tell the person in a firm voice that you will report the act if it happens again.

⇝ If the harassment continues, report the incident to a person in power—the school principal, your section boss, or the personnel office. Realize that you may be questioned or criticized for your accusations, but if someone is making you feel uncomfortable and violating your person, you have the right to stop them from continuing to harass you.

↝ If the incidents become serious (touching you sexually or threatening you), you may decide to press charges. This can be a very difficult choice because you do open yourself up to a lot of attention surrounding an uncomfortable situation. But remember, you are not the one who is wrong.

↝ If the situation escalates into criminal acts such as stalking or personal attacks, go to the police at once and request protection. You may even want to get a court order to keep the person from coming anywhere near you. Consult a lawyer if legal action is needed and keep track of when and how the person is harassing you.

Playing Games

There was a time when only boys used to play team sports while girls cheered them on. In 1972, "Title IX" became law and changed that. This law requires that high schools and colleges that receive federal money spend proportionally equal amounts of money on men's and women's athletic programs. Enforcement has been slow, but young women today win athletic scholarships to colleges, something unheard of when their mothers were in school. It is clear that support in the world of sports has helped women in other areas as well; for example, 80 percent of female managers of Fortune 500 companies have a sports background.

The Military

In 1970, 41,479 women were on military active duty. Since then, that number has steadily increased. In 1995 females in the military numbered over 196,000—about 13 percent of the Army, Air Force, Navy, and Marines.

The increase in the number of women in the military has brought with it an increase in gender-related issues, such as whether or not pregnant women should remain on duty, when a remark between equals is sexual harassment, and when the rough treatment of new female cadets has crossed the line into harassment. A series of sex scandals in 1996 prompted an investigation by Congress. The report that resulted focused on whether training in the armed services should be integrated or segregated by sex. Writing about the situation, Dr. Dorothy H. Rosenke asked, "Is there a comfortable solution to be found?"

"No," Dr. Rosenke answered herself. "Hopefully, in the future," she wrote, "discussions and decisions about initial entry training will be based . . . upon sound research and the military needs of our nation."

The Tree House Syndrome

Women in the workplace often feel that many men have never gotten over the tree house syndrome: "You can't play in my tree house 'cause you're a girl." They say men worry about competing with them for a job and losing control of what has been a "man's world." Consequently, they feel that male bosses do not give them the chance to take jobs that were traditionally performed by men.

"Assumptions that women do not want higher-paying jobs because they prefer to sell baubles, bangles, and beads, or cannot do certain jobs because they require physical work, may be responsible in part for the wage gaps the Bureau of Labor Statistics continues to find."
—Sabra Chartrand,
"Wage Report Sparks Online Duels Between Sexes,"
New York Times, November 9, 1997

Why Change Seems to Have Slowed

Some women today have no desire to climb high on the career ladder. They are split within themselves when it comes to their goals and life choices. They can have powerful, satisfying, well-paying careers. But they may also feel that staying home and rearing children is the best career a woman can have. Because they see that their choices today are much wider than in their grandmother's day, many of them have stopped actively working for equality with men.

Older women, for whom career choices were limited by society, shake their heads. They worked hard to be taken seriously in the workplace and to be able to set their own life goals. They actively fought a society that allowed them to have only unfulfilling jobs outside the home. They wonder why some women today, with so much less discrimination, impose limits on themselves when the opportunities are so readily available.

We've got a generation now who were born with semi-equality. They don't know how it was before, so they think this isn't too bad . . . I get very disgusted with the younger generation of women. We had a torch to pass, and they are just sitting there.
    —Erma Bombeck, writer (as quoted in
    Treasury of Women's Quotations)

"Wait a Minute. I Should Have That Job!"

As women have gained rights, many men think they have lost theirs. When colleges and employers give priority to a female, it may seem to a man like discrimination, even if it is done in the name of balancing a student body or staff.

This year, my son lost out on an internship because he's not female or a minority. Luckily, he managed to get a research fellowship, but he had been counting on the job, and was highly qualified, just not a member of the groups they were targeting. It'll be interesting to see what happens with the swing away from affirmative action—it's a real mess. No one wins, it seems.
    —Rosemary Garr, parent and teacher

Gender issues often arise on the job. How to resolve such problems can be clouded by the point of view people have about the role gender plays.

[Letter to Editor in response to two men claiming sex discrimination by female bosses] . . . *I find it disgusting, the hypocrisy of the feminist management . . . if they were in the same situation as these men are, they would be the first to scream and shout sex discrimination . . . Men need to assert themselves and not be intimidated by these left-wing feminists who are completely anti-male.*
　　　　　　　　　　—*Frederick News-Post,* November 23, 1996

What Can You Do to Cope with Gender Discrimination?

No matter what your point of view, conflict based on gender is a part of life. Awareness of the issues will help you deal with male/female discrimination, but here are some specific tips:

➣ Expect remarks about masculinity when someone catches a man doing what is considered "traditional women's work." Or expect remarks about femininity when a woman does what people believe only men should do. If these remarks are aimed at you, tell that person that this job is no longer "woman's work" or "man's work" and that you do not put limits on yourself or your abilities, or on others and their abilities.

Xenophobia

xenophobia *(zen-uh-fo-bee-uh): Fear or hatred of anything that is strange or foreign.*

Xenophobia

The word xenophobia has it's roots in an ancient Greek word that means "strange." Over time the definition has broadened to mean, "fear of strangers." It now also means fear and hatred towards members of a certain group who are seen as different from the norm. These people most often belong to a different racial or ethnic group.

What Is Racism?

To prefer and to take pride in one's own race is not racist. Racists do not stop with taking pride in their own group. They seek to make themselves superior by putting others down. The examples that first come to mind are well-known groups like the Ku Klux Klan and the Aryan Nation. Today those aforementioned groups have much less power. Still, every race has groups that try to elevate their people with acts of hate against others. They are xenophobic.

Tolerance

One answer to coping with xenophobia is for everyone, regardless of race and ethnic group, to develop tolerance for others.

Often, by learning about someone else's customs, cultural values, and traits, we change our feelings of fear and dislike of others to respect and sometimes even admiration. My lifestyle may be very different from yours, but if you are tolerant and open to learning, you may discover that mine is not better or worse, but just different.

Knowing about and being more tolerant of others' lifestyles helps us better empathize with them.

History of Racism in the United States

The problems of racism date back to the first white settlers who took possession of the land from the Native Americans. Slavery widened the racial divide. Immigrants from around the world who poured into the United States in the early twentieth century were seen as a threat to the establishment. Consequently, laws were passed that denied rights to some people in an effort to maintain the power structure that prevailed at the time.

Where the United States Stands Today

In the United States, issues revolving around racism between blacks and whites seem, in some ways, more positive than they have ever been. In response to the question, "Looking at discrimination in racial terms, have you seen any changes in the last few years?" Writer Sam Fulwood III replied, "Yes, there has been tremendous change. For the better."

He went on to say, "It hasn't gotten to the point where it's perfect. Color matters enormously. We are still a racially stratified and divided society. I think that it should change. I wish that it would. I'm not optimistic.

"We now have people who are not as willing as people were in the '60s to try to create an integrated society, even as we're becoming more integrated. The forces of demographics are making us a much more racially diverse society, while at the same time people seem to be resistant to embracing that diversity."

Racism: Not Just a Black and White Issue

These "forces of demographics" mean racism in the United States can no longer be discussed in terms of black and white. Consider that:

- At the start of the twenty-first century, African Americans make up only 12 percent of the people in the United States ; other minorities are growing at a much faster rate.

- Almost a million immigrants, many of whom are Latino/Latina by birth, enter the United States each year. Asians form the second largest group.

- About 25 percent of Hispanics and 33 percent of Asian Americans marry someone from a race not their own.

↝ The United States Census Bureau introduced 126 possible racial combinations for the year 2000 census.

Fear Keeps Us Standing Still

Many people have noted that fear prevents people from moving in a positive direction. In his book *Waking from the Dream,* Fulwood says that racism, "or the fear of racism, works like gravity. It grounds . . . people's thinking and aspirations."

The attitude "Why try?" is sometimes more harmful than even actual racism. While racism does exist, people's fear of racism can have even worse consequences. That fear can keep them from success. It can prevent them from moving to a better job, house, school, or achieving the goal they dream of. It can destroy their spirit and their dreams.

I am Mexican-American. I know how a four-year-old child feels when he is told to stand aside because white people are served first, how it feels to be told that you have to sit in the back of the church, to be called names both by perfect strangers and kids on the playground, and to be bullied and physically assaulted. How could anyone treat another person that way?

The anguish and despair are like a cancer that eats away that child's spirit.

—Richard Spurgeon

Fear also grounds the thinking of those in power who use old stereotypes. Saying "She got the job because she's

41

a minority," is an easy way for a person to shrug off fears and keep a narrow point of view.

People Fear Change

Many people fear change and prefer the status quo—keeping things as they are. Change means giving up things that we may want to keep and having to adapt to a new situation that we may not like or of which we are unsure.

Some people fear change because it might mean that they will loose their power. Others may think that they will be giving up job opportunities or the ability to get into the university of their choice. Some people may simply fear the need to get to know someone who lives a life that they are not familiar with or is from a country where things are done differently. One example of this is the threat southerners face of not being able to fly the Confederate flag. Southerners who fly a Confederate flag send a message that they want to restore life to the way it was long ago.

"With the removal of the Confederate battle flag at the beginning of this new year, the 2000 session of the General Assembly has the opportunity to deliver a message throughout South Carolina and across this nation, of unification, inclusion, and opportunity for all South Carolinians," [Rock Hill, SC, mayor Doug] Echols said.

South Carolina is the only state that still flies the Confederate flag above its Capitol. Only the Legislature can lower the flag, which was raised in 1962 for the Civil War centennial. However, other than periodic statements from

members of York County's legislative delegation, who mostly back the status quo, elective bodies in York County have been largely silent on this issue.
—Andrew J. Skerritt, *The Herald*, Rock Hill, South Carolina, December 20, 1999

Xenophobia is a vicious circle; People fear those they do not know, but they do not want to know those people because they fear them.

The Power of Diversity

While many people fear diversity and change, other people applaud it.

Would we live our life only gazing at tulips and no other kind of flower, would we refuse to accept the shade of only an oak tree and no other, would we eat only Italian food and no other? How bland and small the world would be. If people live their life as a racist, how bland and small their world is.
—Doug and Jennifer Merson, "Letter to the Editor," *Frederick News-Post*, August 11, 1997

Divided We Fall

Diversity is great, but when it becomes divisive, there's a problem.
—Dr. Jenny Johnson, Professor, University of Maryland University College

In the United States, citizens are expected first and foremost to be loyal to the United States. Many people worry that what has been called excessive ethnocentricity could destroy the United States. They fear that favoring an ethnic group above love of one's own community—the community called the United States—weakens the community. In the past, most first generation immigrants have preferred the ways of their homeland. By the second or third generation, however, regardless of pride in roots, most have learned English and fit in with the local lifestyle. Time will tell if this pattern will continue.

For the first time in my life I attended a naturalization ceremony. One hundred fifty-six people of many races, from forty countries. Some were in their native clothing, others in clothes straight from the mall. They stood there and bravely gave up any allegiance to their home country. They vowed to fight for this country, if asked, and swore to protect the Constitution. My spouse and I had tears in our eyes. I can't imagine having the courage to walk away from a homeland, to go to a new country, unable to speak the language, gambling on an uncertain dream of a better life in a new world. I had felt a lot of prejudice toward immigrants, but I now saw them in a different light.
—Claudine Wirths

Coping with the New Racial and Ethnic Diversity

No matter how you feel about the racial makeup of the

United States at the start of the twenty-first century, you will have to learn to cope with it.

The conversation about race in our society is very much focused on the lack of respect of one race for another. We need to realize that our racial history sets us up to be suspicious of each other. Only the least aware among us still believes that one race is superior to another. But African Americans are still suspicious that whites are looking down on them and whites are still suspicious that African Americans hate all whites because of past history. A healthier way to approach race relations is to acknowledge our terrible racial history, accept these suspicions as all too natural, if uncomfortable to deal with, and face the need to focus on exploring areas of mutual interest one person at a time.
—Carl Kruhm, Jr., retired teacher

Whatever your race, coping will be easier if you focus on someone first as an individual, not as a member of a race. Get to know the man or woman behind their outward appearance.

The Future

"But what comes next? While civil rights forces may be at a crossroads, maybe America stands there, too. The old paradigms need to be challenged. Our old ideas about 'race' need remaking. Now's a chance for exciting breakthroughs—if we are bold enough to reach for the ring."
—Joe R. Hicks, Executive Director of the Multicultural Collaborative,
Los Angeles Times, July 20, 1997 (online edition)

God? Jehovah? Allah? G-D? Atheist?

There is no more deeply felt emotion than religious belief, and our beliefs motivate us. Inspired by their religion, people throughout history have done some of humankind's greatest and most noble acts. They have also, in the name of religion, committed some of the worst acts of discrimination.

What Is Religion?

Religion, in its broadest sense, is a way to give meaning to life, death, and nature. Religion requires believing in a power greater than human power. Most religious people worship that greater power.

Anthropologists, those who study how humans live, have shown that nearly every culture on earth has had some form of religion. People have worshiped a force, or power, which they have often believed resided in things such as animals, trees, the sun, the moon, gold, or real and unreal people. This does not mean that they worshiped those things. Those who throw gifts into a river do not worship the river. They are sacrificing to the spirit in the river.

Speaking to the Same God in a Different Language

Today, most people who are religious participate in one of

the many large and small organized religions. Most of us join a religious group with which we feel comfortable—often the one to which we were exposed at an early age. We join because we seek to be with others who have the same values and share the same world view.

Rabbi David Wolpe says, in *Teaching Your Children about God,* " . . . different people worship the same God, but they use a different religious language, just as we can speak the same messages to each other all over the world, but in different spoken languages."

If some people at a party begin speaking a different language, the others soon feel alienated. That seems to be what happens when people speak to God in a different way; others do not understand, feel left out, and judge that difference in a negative way.

The Problem

Religions are prejudicial almost by definition. We do not join a group intending to leave others out. But the more we participate in one religion and as our own beliefs become stronger, the more prejudice we may feel against those who prescribe to a different faith. Likewise, we may encounter more discrimination from other religious groups when we identify ourselves as members of a particular religious group.

➪ The Roman Catholic Church teaches that Catholicism is the true Christian faith. Is that an act of discrimination against Baptists?

➪ Christmas carols play endlessly in the stores and on

47

radio and TV during the month of December. Is that an act of discrimination against Jewish people?

☞ Most calendars in the United States leave off the important holy days in the Muslim faith but put in Christmas and Hanukkah. Is that an act of discrimination against Muslims?

Politics and Religion

Politics and religion are frequently entangled when a political leader supports a particular belief. This oftentimes leads to discrimination against groups with different beliefs.

This idea of the "right" belief ("orthodoxy") has varied from religion to religion, from time period to time period, and from country to country. It has been especially strong in Christianity from the third century to today. Some Christian rulers have killed non-believers, gone to war to convert whole countries, and found ways to destroy the livelihood of those who did not follow their beliefs.

Christians also fight among themselves. Most people in and out of Northern Ireland today wonder why Catholics and Protestants continue their centuries-long fight. Why, people wonder, in the twenty-first century, can't a lasting peace be achieved? Many feel desire for power, not religious fervor, is now at the heart of the problem.

Discrimination in the name of religion is not limited to Christians. In World War II, thousands of Japanese killed Americans or died for their Emperor, the spiritual head of Shintoism. Today in Iran, followers of the Ayatollah fight rival believers, and in Israel the Jews and Arabs are still at war despite many attempts at peace.

The Nature of Believing

Almost every religious belief system carries with it strong statements about how a person should live his or her life. A true believer chooses those statements to guide his or her way of life and renounces any other. In many religions the believer thinks other ways of life are wrong. Taken to an extreme, this means that followers think that those who believe otherwise should be destroyed or converted so that they too will live the "right" way. In other words, many believers are prejudiced and believe that their way is how everyone should live. This prejudice sets the stage for discrimination.

What If You Don't Believe?

People who are unsure about the idea of a supreme power are called agnostics. Freely translated, that means, "I'm not certain about what to believe, if anything." Often these people join a religious group like the Unitarian Universalists, who stress inquiry and study rather than a rigid belief system. Or they join a more traditional religious group and go along with the practices even if they do not always believe every word said or written.

Those who have clearly decided that there is no supreme being are called atheists (*a* meaning "without" and *theist* meaning "God"—in other words, they believe that there is no supreme power and that life is just this existence). There are societies and groups for atheists to join. Atheists were instrumental in removing required prayers from public schools in the United States. This move was supported by many nonatheists because they believed it might make religious discrimination less pervasive.

Some people believe so deeply in God that they actively reject people who are openly atheist. Christian groups strongly opposed to non-believers carry on a long tradition of discrimination against them. There was a time in England when, unless you swore you believed in God, you could not be a witness in court. That, in fact, seems mild compared to the fate of many in England and elsewhere who were drowned, boiled in oil, beheaded, or burned at the stake for not adhering to the established religious view.

Religious Discrimination

We have come a long way in tolerating the views of others where religion is concerned, but religious discrimination continues to be an issue. When it comes to religion, many people casually commit acts that hurt, even though they may be low-level acts of discrimination.

My husband was talking with some friends with whom he rode to work. One of them made a crude remark which made fun of Jews. The others in the car laughed. Since my husband has a very Italian last name, the man didn't know that John converted to Judaism when we married.
—A teacher in Buffalo, New York.

Some people use religion as a reason to commit high-level acts of discrimination.

Hoping to catch the vandals responsible for scrawling anti-Semitic graffiti on a Lancaster synagogue, the Los Angeles County Board of Supervisors is offering a $5,000 reward . . . Sometime after midnight January 23, graffiti vandals struck Temple Beth Knesset Bamidbar in Lancaster. Using a black marker, the vandals scrawled swastikas, pentagrams, and hate-related messages on the synagogue walls and door.

—Bart Weitzel, *Antelope Valley* (CA) *Press,*
February 3, 2000

Dating Someone of a Different Religion

So what about dating or going out with someone who has no religious affiliation or is not of your faith?

In your early years, going out with someone of a different faith may not matter much. However, the older you are and the more ready you may be for marriage and a family, the harder and more personal this question becomes. Family members who have strong belief systems may try to control your choice.

There are many religions that, by their rituals and beliefs, strongly object to members marrying anyone of a different faith who will not convert. Their reasons are many, but they mainly come down to the impact on family life when children become involved. Faith is a deeply held belief and we do not easily change our deeply held feelings. If these feelings involve rules and rituals for the "right" life, we cannot easily give them up or even agree on a compromise. Many couples have found this out the hard way after they have married and had children.

The experience of Malcolm Forbes, the owner and publisher of the business magazine *Forbes*, is one example of how mixing faiths within a marriage can be difficult. A TV biography about Forbes reported that his father was a Presbyterian and his mother Roman Catholic. All told, his parents had five children. They decided to baptize the first one Catholic, the second Presbyterian, and so on. Since Malcolm was the third child, he was brought up Catholic. Later he learned that his mother had secretly had the others baptized Catholic as well because she feared for their souls if they were not. In time, she and her husband separated because of other differences but they never divorced, because of her Catholic beliefs.

Compromise in religious matters is more likely between people with similar beliefs—say Baptists and Methodists—than it is between major faiths, such as Muslims and Jews. People have married across faiths and made the marriage and family work, but a difference in faith can add to problems in a marriage.

Coping with Religious Discrimination

⇝ For minor, low-level acts of discrimination, you can choose to ignore it or to confront it. If someone tries to bully you, walk away. If you think the person simply did not realize that what was said or done was hurtful to you, talk with him or her. If you have a religious leader, talk to this person to release your feelings of anger or depression about being a target.

⇝ For more serious, mid-level acts, consult with one

of the organizations dedicated to dealing with religious discrimination.

☞ For very serious high-level acts, like a cross-burning in your yard, hate messages sprayed on your house, or physical violence against you, call the police. Most communities have laws against hate crimes. See the Appendix for how to report such acts.

☞ Find out if your place of worship or community has group meetings or workshops that help people cope with discrimination. If not, encourage starting such programs. The guidelines of the Anti-Defamation League of B'nai B'rith are good ones to follow in describing incidents to a support group. The guidelines suggest that you define the acts in terms of either harassment (verbal or written threat, physical assault) or vandalism (attacks on property, such as arson, destruction, defacement). You should also refer to the Appendix for how to report such acts.

Practicing Tolerance When You're Strongly Committed to a Particular Faith

How can we be true to our own faith and yet relate to others without committing acts of discrimination? The Reverend Barbara Sears, an Episcopal deacon, answers the question this way: "We relate to each other on many different levels. Sometimes we relate on one level, sometimes on another. People (especially friends) can agree not to relate on the level of religious beliefs." In other words, most of the time we can focus on the many parts of life that we share and keep private certain areas of life we do not share.

In summary, we can keep our acts of discrimination to the least hurtful level if we truly treat others as we want them to treat us.

To Think About

☞ Make a list of all the people you know, family, neighbors, teachers, and friends. List the religion to which each belongs. How important is their religious belief to you in your friendship with them? Why? Does it ever cause you to turn away from them?

☞ In the United States, coins bear the words "In God We Trust." The president of the United States has always taken the oath of office with one hand on a Christian Bible. Yet, the United States was founded on freedom of religion. Should a president be able to take the oath of office without his or her hand on the Bible?

Abled, Disabled, and Enabled

People with disabilities, especially severe disabilities, have been discriminated against throughout history. The ancient Greeks left them to die on mountaintops. Until recent years, families would shut them up in the family home or in an institution.

Today, a number of federal laws seek to prevent discrimination against people with disabilities. The Americans with Disabilities Act clearly says that people with disabilities cannot be discriminated against. Most people today understand disabilities better and realize that people with disabilities deserve the same rights as everybody else. Most schools have students with disabilities who attend classes with regular education students. Many workers with disabilities put in a full day's work.

Unfortunately, many people with disabilities believe they are still discriminated against in the workplace because employers will not give them a chance to excel, or because workplaces are inaccessible.

Not only is finding a job hard, but simply moving around the world outside their homes is not easy for many people with disabilities. Those who are physically disabled may not have proper access to many public and private buildings. The long sweep of marble stairs leading up to the Lincoln Memorial in Washington is beautiful, but quite daunting to a person in a wheelchair.

Kind and Cruel Are the Same Coin

The ways in which people discriminate against those with disabilities range from low-level to high-level acts. Sometimes discrimination can be meant as kindness, and other times it is just cruel.

➴ Discrimination through kindness: The person with the disability is treated too gently, too sweetly. He or she is not allowed to be independent to the greatest extent possible. Thinking, speaking, and doing for someone cannot help him or her get and hold a job, live on his or her own, and do the adult things done by most of us.

➴ Discrimination that is cruel: The person with the disability is ignored, made fun of, rejected, or taken advantage of. In high-level acts, the person may be physically or mentally mistreated.

Both kinds of discrimination hurt. You could say people who treat someone with a disability too kindly mean well, but the long-term effects of too much kindness are still harmful.

Types of Disabilities

Disabilities can range from minor to severe and can show themselves in a number of ways or, as is often the case, they can be hidden. Not everyone with emotional problems, for example, gets loud and violent; some people become severely depressed; still others become afraid to leave the house. Someone with developmental disabilities may be well-spoken so that you would not immediately notice they have a disability; someone else may have trouble expressing even basic needs.

Below are thumbnail sketches of the major areas of disability and tips to help you empathize in an accepting and acceptable way with those who have them.

Vision, Speech, and Hearing Impairment

He couldn't tell [the salesperson] he has been deaf since infancy, or that he struggles to read or write, or that he has little command of English or Spanish.

Hurwitz [sign language teacher] said: "It's the ethical and legal duty of these salesmen, when dealing with a hearing and verbally impaired person, to insist that he return with someone who can help him understand what he is buying."

—John M. Glionna, "Advocate for the Disabled
Seeks a U-Turn on Car Deal,"
Los Angeles Times, March 22, 1997

Hearing

Hearing loss ranges from slight to total, deafness. People with problems in hearing that cannot be corrected with aids or other devices may sign with their hands or may read lips. Someone who reads lips is better able to mix with hearing people, but lip-reading is a hard skill to learn and many people have not been taught this technique.

In most cases, the earlier and more severe their hearing loss, the more trouble people have learning to speak and read, even if they have average or above intelligence. Here are some suggestions to follow when communicating with someone with hearing loss:

☞ Speak slowly. Look at the person and speak as clearly as you can. Do not cover your mouth with your hand when you speak. Do not shout, but move closer to the person's ear or microphone. The microphone may be on the person's chest but is more likely in or on the ear.

☞ Make a sign of writing with your fingers and offer the person pencil and paper.

☞ If you are dealing with a person with profound hearing loss who signs, learn a few signs, such as "Hello" and "Sorry" and "Can I help you?"

Speech

People with severe speech problems are often helped by the use of equipment that speaks for them. This equipment may simply be a board with drawings that the person points to. Or it can be a small computer. With most devices the person also needs some help and patience on your part to be understood.

☞ If someone has trouble speaking, do not assume the person is also deaf.

☞ Assure the person that you want to understand. Whether the person is using his or her own voice to speak or using a piece of equipment, tell the person to take his or her time.

☞ If someone stutters, being nervous often makes the problem worse. Smile and say that you are in no hurry. Do not tease or poke fun, imitate speech, or fill in words.

Vision

Many of us wear glasses or contact lenses. When vision loss cannot be corrected and impairs daily life, it becomes a disability.

> ↩ If someone with a vision problem asks for directions, guide the person by lightly touching their elbow with the palm of your hand. Holding their hand is not appropriate when you do not know them.

> ↩ Do not approach a person who is blind and make bodily contact without speaking first.

Physical

The design of Franklin Delano Roosevelt's statue in Washington, D.C., stirred much debate about how he should be shown. When Roosevelt was president from 1933 to 1945, he didn't want people to see him in his wheelchair for fear that he would be discriminated against. He thought that if people saw that he was unable to walk, they would consider him a weak and helpless person. In designing his statue, the question arose as to whether he should be shown as he was or as he was perceived by the public. In those days, news photographers did not pry into, but rather protected, the lives of public figures.

The statue was built and shows Roosevelt in a flowing cape, which he did in fact wear. Only the small wheels on the back of the wheelchair can be seen. In noting that FDR gave the United States the strength to win World War II, Bill Bradley, on CBS News, Saturday, August 9,

1997, said, "This so-called disabled man put America back on its feet."

Like Roosevelt, a major concern for those with physical disabilities is the myth that, because they have physical problems, something is also wrong with them mentally. Clearly, this is a huge misconception.

As with all disabilities, the way in which a physical disability shows itself ranges widely. Here are some suggestions for interacting with someone with a physical disability.

↪ Help the person only if help is asked for or is clearly badly needed.

↪ Give the person room. Maneuvering a wheelchair, crutches, or walker or simply walking can require more space. For the same reason, do not park too close to a handicapped parking space. And never use a handicapped parking space unless you or someone for whom you are driving qualifies.

Developmental Delay (Mental Retardation)

The director of the group home helped the four young adults with mental retardation settle down to eat. While they happily munched away at their burgers and fries, he watched other people in the fast food restaurant leave the counter and move to tables. Several started toward their table, looked at the group, and moved to a table further away. "Why can't people at least sit near us?" the director thought.

You may see people with developmental disabilities anywhere. Reacting to someone with a developmental disability takes some special coping tips.

When interacting with people with mental retardation, be mindful of being too friendly. Caregivers often have a hard time teaching those with developmental disabilities not to be too friendly. If you are too friendly to someone with a developmental delay, you give them the message that talking, touching, or even going off to shop with strangers is okay. For their safety, teachers and caregivers do not want those with developmental delays to get that message. The fear is that harm will come to them if they talk too readily to strangers.

When you are talking with someone with developmental delays, here are some other things to avoid.

⇒ Do not yell. Speaking louder does not help someone with mental retardation understand. Use simple words and short sentences.

⇒ Never touch. They may try to hug you as a way of thanking you for being friendly to them. Simply pull away gently. Giving hugs to strangers isn't what most people do, and those with developmental delays should not, either.

Emotional Problems

When Glenda began preparing her speech three weeks ago, she felt elated. She wrote feverishly and practiced happily in front of a mirror. Then her mood changed. She felt blue and sad as she dragged herself through each day. On the day she was to give the speech, she looked over her notes. "This doesn't make sense," she thought. "I can't say that." Feeling great despair, she quickly wrote a new

*speech. When the teacher gave her a D, she felt useless.
"My life is terrible," she thought.*

People with emotional problems show many different signs. Some have outbursts in which they lose control of how they act and what they say. Others sink into long periods of despair and depression. Emotional problems, like any disability, also range in severity. If you know someone who has emotional outbursts:

☞ Encourage them to get help. If they refuse, talk to a counselor, the staff at a place of worship, or social worker about how best to cope with the problem.

☞ Do not make excuses for them or be overly protective. If you do, you are helping them learn to use their disability to manipulate others. You are not helping them cope with their emotional life.

When dealing with people who are depressed:

☞ Listen attentively and encourage them to talk about their feelings.

☞ Encourage them to get medical and psychological help. Doctors can help most people overcome depression.

Learning Problems

Learning disabilities are often not visible.

Many people with learning disabilities have trouble with reading, writing, and math. They also may have trouble thinking in an orderly way and sitting or standing still.

They may daydream, be prone to accidents, and be easily distracted.

When dealing with a person you know has learning disabilities:

- Give simple directions, one step at a time.

- Be sure that you have the person's full attention if you want him or her to do something or know something.

- Use calendars, charts, tape recorders, and color-coded lists to help the person remember tasks and commitments.

Interacting with Anyone with a Disability

Here are some general ideas that will keep you from discriminating against people who have disabilities.

- Treat the person as you would others. For instance, if someone is having trouble opening a door, you would help. But don't step in to take over for someone if he or she doesn't need the help.

- Avoid using terms like "crazy" to describe behavior. Instead, describe the behavior you saw, such as "talked a lot."

- Respond directly to the person with the problem, not their caregiver.

- Look the person in the eye when you talk.

- Do not be put off by the person's problem or appearance.

63

Institutional Discrimination: Discrimination by Default

Institutional discrimination can be a harder concept to grasp than personal discrimination, but its practice is just as widespread.

Institutional discrimination occurs within groups. The groups may be organizations, such as companies where we work or clubs where we play, or they may be institutions, such as schools, banks, government offices, and places of worship. In this chapter the general term institution means any formal organization, establishment, or company. Since groups are made up of people, institutional discrimination is based on personal feelings of prejudice that lead to group customs, rules, or regulations. These can result in discrimination.

The institution may or may not intend to discriminate. Like much discrimination, we may never know the motives behind the act. But we can often see the results. In many companies, for instance, decisions and networking happen on the golf course. If the men play at a "men only" club, the women in the company are shut out and are not likely to move up the leadership ranks because they are not "insiders."

You may have heard the term default used in the sense that a team wins by default when the other team cannot perform. Here we will use the term default as it is used in computer lingo.

Understanding Computer Defaults

Default—value, action, or setting that the computer sys-tem assumes unless the user gives an explicit instruction to the contrary.
    —InfoGenie User's Guide, Casady & Greene, Inc.

A computer program does some things by default. In computer lingo this means that certain commands are built into the software program. The computer follows those commands forever unless you tell it to do something different.

Let us say you open a word-processing program and begin writing. When the designers developed the pro-gram, they set the width of the margins and how the let-ters and numbers would look on the screen.

If you like the look of what you see on the screen, no problem. But suppose you do not like the size of the let-ters or how dark they are or where they will show up when you print the page. Then you must figure out how to make a change in the default settings.

Institutional Default Settings

In the same way, institutions have default settings. Institu-tions are set up with certain rules, regulations, customs, and habits that direct their day-to-day running. These become the default settings of that institution. You can recognize a default setting when someone says, "We've always done it that way." Or, "That's how things are done around here."

A simple example is when a company has the custom of never firing an old employee even if he or she is no longer a good employee. This practice discriminates against new workers because there is no room for them to move up.

Is This Discrimination?

We said institutional discrimination is harder to grasp and understand than personal discrimination. It can also be far harder to recognize. Would you call the following acts of discrimination?

⇔ A local health department writes a bulletin to warn citizens about the threat of a disease carried by ticks. The bulletin is filled with scientific words that an average person cannot read or understand.

⇔ A golf club has a policy of not allowing women to tee off during certain hours and on weekends.

⇔ A single mother takes a part-time job so she can leave the welfare rolls. She would like to have health insurance for herself and her children, but she cannot afford it. Her employer refuses to increase the number of her work hours because the company would then have to pay for her health insurance.

Directly or Indirectly, You Are Part of the Default Settings

So where do you fit in? Each of us is part of institutional discrimination because we, as a part of society belong to many organizations and institutions. Many of these entities are choked with discriminatory practices.

For example, have you ever asked what your bank's policy is about making loans? You might find that all the money goes to support a highly discriminatory system that makes money for wealthy people and the bank, but has a strict policy for low-income families.

As you gain insight into how institutional discrimination works, you will no doubt think of other cases that involve you personally. In the next case, the people of the town did not know they were involved until the issue was made public, but the entire town was soon involved one way or another. Although this took place in the southwest United States, a similar incident could happen in any town.

Two Discriminating Teachers versus Institutional Discrimination

Patsy and Nadine Cordova are Chicana sisters who grew up and lived in the small town of Vaughn, New Mexico. They both taught in the local school, which only has about seventy students in grades seven through twelve. These teachers wanted to make their students, almost all Chicano, more aware of their own history. The Cordovas chose materials they felt gave a view of history that would make students proud of their heritage. They also wanted the students to recognize and question the biases presented in traditional history books which are generally always written from the European point of view.

The superintendent of schools and the school board told the Cordovas to stop using the new materials. They felt such materials generated racism because they created a stereotype of Europeans only as conquerors and gold-grabbers in the New World.

When the teachers got their orders, they abided by them. But they then turned to a kit of materials called *The Shadow of Hate: A History of Intolerance in America,* published by Teaching Tolerance of the Southern Poverty Law Center. The Cordovas asked for approval to use it and, when they did not get an answer after a few days, they began to use parts of the kit anyway.

Action was quickly taken against the teachers that charged that they were still teaching a biased, anti-European view of history. There were also counter-charges from the townspeople that the Cordova's were actually teaching tolerance for all people. The matter came to a head when the teachers were abruptly fired and given ten minutes to clear out of their classrooms.

The above is a very short description of what happened, based on an article in *Teacher* magazine (August/September 1997). The *Albuquerque Journal* reported (Thursday, November 19, 1998) that the teachers received a $520,000 settlement that they would share with their attorneys and the American Civil Liberties Union. In this article, Nadine Cordova is quoted as saying, "At the root of this was that we were teaching Chicano studies and they didn't want us teaching it. [But] it was complicated. It's not just one simple issue that was involved in this."

While this story is indeed complex, it shows institutional discrimination in action. Teachers are supposed to have the freedom of speech granted them in the Bill of Rights of the United States Constitution. The fact is that school boards and administrators have always been able to control what teachers must teach. Often for very good reasons, the boards do not like changes that make parents and students uneasy or unhappy. But clearly, there are times when changes should be made.

Can You Change an Institution?

If you want to make changes in a computer's default settings, it can be easy, if you know the program. On the other hand, if you do not know much about the program or how that computer system works, making changes could be very difficult. You may need help but it might be hard to find. You may even have trouble finding out if the problem rests with you, the program, or the way the program works.

If you want to make a change in the default settings of an institution, you are faced with the same situation. If you do not know how the system works, you could be in real trouble. You may be confused, and want help. If you ask for help, you may not get the help you need. You may not even be able to find out if the problem rests with you, society, or the way the institution's system works

How to Cope with Institutional Discrimination

If you wish to cope with institutional discrimination, you need to be able to recognize it. Look into the different organizations with which you are involved. Read through a local newspaper. You can regularly find cases of institutional discrimination if you are mindful of it.

For instance, the Food and Drug Administration has at last moved to force drug companies to include young women in studies of new medicines. For years, tests for new drugs did not include women of childbearing age.

The government and drug companies said they had fears that if any of the women got pregnant, the drugs would harm the baby. But the policy also kept women with life-threatening diseases away from studies that held the hope of help. Many women no doubt died because they were not given the opportunity to use these drugs. Another, probably worse problem was also perpetuated in this situation: doctors applied the results of the studies to all patients, working under the assumption that men and women reacted to drugs in the same way. Now that there is more testing done on both men and women, it has become clear that this assumption is not always true, and has certainly and unknowingly caused problems for many women in the past.

Once you start your investigating, you will see cases of institutional discrimination all around you. Sometimes there is a tendency to blame the victim; the system is only protecting itself and the individual should learn to live with the rules. Many times institutional discrimination is masked as good intentions and is not blatant or obvious discrimination. Many times it is justified as being necessary for the greater good of all people involved. Other times a situation is disguised as the "routine way of handling that problem," that is, the person enforcing the rule is only "doing their job" and following the rules that have been handed down to them. The fault of the discrimination lies in "the institution." The bottom line—it is still discrimination and it can be changed. Let your opinions be heard. Institutions are made up of people. Find out who has the power to change discriminatory policies and let them know how you feel.

We all are part of the larger system. The problems of discrimination that exist in society belong to all of us. True, none of us can hope to solve all the world's problems, but if we feel strongly about a certain issue, each of us has the right and the power to try to change it.

One Person Can Make a Difference

If you wonder whether one person can make a difference, consider John Boyd, a Virginia farmer. He knew that, while the number of all farms in the United States dropped by only 14 percent in the 1980s, the number of African American–owned farms dropped by more than 40 percent. Over the years, hundreds of African American farmers have charged the United States Department of Agriculture (USDA) and its local agents with biased loan practices. Boyd found that, of the hundreds of complaints against the USDA by African American farmers, only two had been settled. Even though top USDA officials admitted that loan requests by African American farmers were often denied or delayed until the farm had to be sold, little action resulted.

Boyd wanted action. He formed the National Black Farmers Association. At rallies, in interviews that attracted media attention, on television, and in newspapers, Boyd preached his message. Others who think black farmers deserve fair, equal, and timely treatment have joined him.

Through hard work, networking with other African American farmers across the United States, and using the media to press his points, Boyd hopes to make the system admit its mistakes. He also hopes his efforts will help him and other African American farmers keep their farms.

71

So when you think you may be encountering institutional discrimination, try, like Boyd, to understand what is going on. If you believe the institution's actions are wrong and you want to move ahead, take intelligent, well-thought out action to make changes and to make the system work properly. If you make your case clearly and strongly, others may join you, as they have joined Boyd.

Or you may proudly stand alone in what you do, as did one white elected leader in Alabama. He attended a ceremony to honor a white man who gave his life in the blacks' struggle for civil rights in the 1960s.

The town square of Hayneville, Alabama, with a monument to Confederate dead and a courthouse built by slaves, added a monument honoring Jonathan Daniels, a twenty-six-year-old from New England who was shot to death in 1965 by a white man angered by Daniels and other civil rights protesters. "We haven't made the most of the sacrifices of Jonathan Daniels and others who laid down their lives," said Ruby Sales, who was a seventeen-year-old black demonstrator with Daniels, who was white, when he was shot. She said Daniels moved her aside . . . to save her life.

[The article goes on to note that] "only one white elected public official was on hand" for the ceremony.
—Los Angeles Times, August 24, 1997

Discrimination and the Law

A Realtor is required by law and/or the National Association of Realtors code of Ethics to treat all parties in a property transaction fairly without regard to race, color, religion, national origin, ancestry, sex, age, marital status, sexual orientation, presence of children, familial status, source of income, or physical or mental handicaps. If you feel you have been treated unfairly, please contact the Broker.
—from "Some Information Relative to the Purchase of Real Estate," Montgomery County (MD) Association of Realtors, Inc., 1993

It's the Law

Not only is discrimination against the law in renting or buying a home, but also, it is against the law:

☞ In getting a job;

☞ In choosing a place of worship;

☞ In attending school or college;

☞ In getting medical care.

"Wait a minute," you may be saying. "If discrimination is against the law, why aren't the jails filled to the top? I see discrimination every day."

73

True, but not all acts of discrimination are against the law. What's more, illegal acts must be proved in the courts if someone is to be held accountable and punished—not an easy task. There are even some laws that support discrimination. In fact, such laws were common in past years. Many people alive today remember when the law kept blacks from eating in whites-only restaurants in the South.

Of course, a law cannot force people to change their point of view. But it can act as a huge nudge to stop society from discriminating, with the hope that eventually it will also change people's points of view.

The Good Old Days?

Over the centuries, many different groups have been the target of laws that discriminated against them. These targeted groups have shifted throughout history as people have learned more and changed their prejudices. Here are two of many examples we could have chosen:

 In Europe during the Middle Ages, people with visible health problems, such as leprosy, were banned from living with the rest of society. They were outcasts. They had no way to earn a living. They had to rely on the charity of family and friends to survive.

 In the mid-1800s people were starving in Ireland. Many Irish families sailed to America and went to the big cities in search of jobs. Their vast numbers and willingness to work at low pay made other workers fear they would lose their jobs. Some people tried to get laws passed that would slow down the numbers of Irish coming to this country.

We chose these two very different examples to make a point. As we noted earlier when we talked about racial discrimination, the basis for most legal discrimination is also fear. Once people learned that leprosy and other medical problems could be treated, fear subsided. When people were still able to get jobs even with many Irish people immigrating, fear again subsided.

What's the Problem?

So why don't we pass laws and stop all discrimination? First, remember viewpoint? Not everyone views discrimination the same way. Some people, for example, believe that laws forbidding sex between people of the same gender are for the public good. Other people think that what adults do in private is their own business and such laws discriminate against gays and lesbians. Almost every law has some people for it and some against it based on their point of view.

Second, some laws against discrimination cannot be supported by the Constitution. Laws that would ban an individual's right to freedom of speech are examples of this.

Third, it would be impossible to get everyone to agree on how such laws should be enforced and what to do if someone breaks the law. No one has yet come up with laws that deal equally with everyone.

Groups of people are still discriminated against through

the legal system. Let us look at some of those groups and their problems.

What Class Are You In?

The people of the United States like to think of this country as a classless society, but the country is generally divided into three income classes—high, middle, and low.

Many of our tax laws favor people with high incomes. The result is discrimination against the poor. This discrimination may be direct but more often is indirect.

An example of indirect discrimination is how schools are funded. Let's say both wealthy and poor neighborhoods get the same amount of public funds to buy computers for their schools. The poorer parents cannot add money to that fund, so children in their schools might have less and lower quality equipment. The wealthy families, however, could donate money to their local schools for computer use so that their children would have state-of-the-art equipment.

This indirect discrimination is compounded when the children of both classes move into the job world. The high-paying jobs go to people who are computer-literate. The lower-paying jobs go to the students who were poorly trained. Losing out on good jobs keeps them where they are and sometimes knocks them further down the economic ladder.

An Old Problem: Aging

A Profile of Older Americans: 1999, prepared by the Administration on Aging of the United States Department of Health and Human Services, and the American Association of Retired Persons (AARP) reported that 12.7 percent of the population is aged sixty-five or older. By 2030, the report goes on to say, people sixty-five and over will make up 20 percent of the total population.

Ageism is a different problem from racism or sexism. Unlike sex or skin color, our age is constantly changing. Although those not yet age sixty-five know they will one day be in that age group, the problems of age discrimination seem distant and obscure.

To older people, however, the problems are close and real. In their day-to-day lives, many feel they are discriminated against. They report they are often treated with disrespect, made to feel threatened, yelled at and given gestures while driving, treated with impatience, short-changed in stores, denied the right to make decisions within the community, and ignored by those who are younger.

One form of discrimination that older people commonly experience is job discrimination. The Age Discrimination in Employment Act covers companies with more than twenty employees and was written to protect workers over age forty. Although it was passed back in 1967, discrimination against older workers is still a problem.

Young people often shrug and wonder why people who could retire do not want to. Like most of us, older people want to be independent, which often means having a job. Of the 3.4 million people aged sixty-five and older, about one of every six (17 percent) can be labeled poor or near poor. Many older workers are let go, passed over for promotions, or not hired because the employer wants someone who looks younger.

The question is often asked, "Won't older workers take jobs away from younger workers or keep others from moving up?" On the AARP "On the Issues" (http://www.aarp.org/ontheissues) Web site, the AARP calls such statements, "an empty argument used to justify outmoded stereotypes about older men and women." First, the AARP notes, younger workers are seeking entry-level jobs, not those usually held by older workers. Second, in today's job market many jobs are unfilled.

Being old or poor are not the only prejudices with which people must cope.

Issues of Sexual Preferences and Identity

Today, public attitudes toward gays and lesbians range from acceptance of their lifestyle to violent rejection and high-level acts of discrimination. An FBI report shows hate crimes committed against people because of their sexual orientation increased from 767 in 1992 to 1,260 in 1998. These numbers show only hate crimes actually reported and forwarded by states to the FBI. There are certainly many more incidents that go unreported. Even so, for 1998 this number represents the third highest number of hate crimes reported. Only those reported for race (4,321) and religion (1,390) were higher.

One reason gays and lesbians are a targeted group is because laws do not exist to protect them. Hate crime based on sexual orientation is not a punishable federal offense unless it occurs on federal property. Less than half the states in the United States have hate crime laws.

In addition, sexual acts between same gender couples

are forbidden by law in many states. Even more complex is the issue of gays and lesbians forming long-term unions that are recognized by the state.

"Love and Marriage. They Go Together Like a Horse and Carriage . . . "

Many gay and lesbian couples want the legal right to get married. This has caused a legal fire-storm. Some people feel marriage is not just a legal contract but a moral and religious issue. They say the goal of a marriage is for the couple to have children and raise a family. Therefore, gays and lesbians should not marry.

Gay and lesbian couples and their supporters say they should not be denied the economic, legal, and emotional stability of marriage. They point out that many gays and lesbians bring up their own children by a previous marriage and adopt children.

Gay and lesbian issues are far from resolved in the courts. However, many companies now accept same-sex partners for health benefits.

Discrimination against gays and lesbians was strong before AIDS came along. But when that virus entered the United States and infected many in the gay population, discrimination against them became more open and volatile and raised new legal issues.

The AIDS Issue

AIDS is a deadly disease and has spread well beyond the gay community. AIDS does not discriminate. Medical progress seems promising, but discrimination against AIDS patients has occurred in schools and in the workplace. Here are some of the questions people have raised:

☞ Should a teacher with AIDS be hired to teach young children?

☞ Should a boy with AIDS be on the school wrestling team?

☞ Should the quality and type of health care for a person with AIDS depend on how he or she got the virus?

The debates over AIDS are not likely to cease until a cure is discovered for the virus. But discrimination against people with serious diseases does not stop with AIDS.

Genetics

Researchers who are searching for the causes of cancer and other diseases are looking to the field of genetics. Doctors believe many of us are born with one or more genes that may lead to certain types of life-threatening diseases. These discoveries raise legal questions, which could give way to more institutional discrimination, such as:

☞ Will insurance companies require certain genetic tests?

☞ Will insurance companies refuse to insure people with certain test results?

☞ Will employers discriminate in hiring?

Prisoners and Ex-Prisoners

For many years much medical research has been done on prisoners. The thinking was twofold: (1) the prisoners paid a debt back to society, and (2) because the testing was controlled, the results could be trusted. Some people still think medical research on prisoners is a good idea. Some say it violates civil rights because the prisoners feel they have to go along with the research if they want to win parole. Today, there is still no agreement on this, but laws have been passed to be sure that prisoners know and understand the research before they agree to be part of it.

One problem is that in the United States, we have never come to terms with how we feel about people who are jailed for breaking the law.

- Should a murderer who will be in jail for life get a needed kidney or heart transplant?

- Are jails and prisons intended to punish people or to rehabilitate them to be better people?

- Once they have been punished (or rehabilitated), should we forgive them and wipe out their records?

We tend to discriminate more against someone who has been caught than we do against someone who gets away with breaking the law. People laugh when friends drive home a bit tipsy, but then are outraged when someone gets caught driving drunk. What does that say about how we really feel?

Class also enters into discrimination against those accused of a crime. Educated, wealthy people are less likely to get caught and can afford good lawyers when they do. The problems most ex-cons face in employment are serious. Many employers will not hire ex-cons especially if the ex-con comes from a low-income class.

Upper-income ex-cons are more likely to be rehired or not lose their jobs at all. The mayor of the District of Columbia, Marion Barry, was reelected mayor as soon as he got out of prison for using drugs.

The Law Is a Double-Edged Sword

More and more minority groups turn to the law as a way to cope with problems of discrimination. They may find, however, that the laws work against them.

Sadly, no one can predict, before a law is passed, how the law will be enforced and what problems may arise because of the new law. For example, many people who fought for affirmative action laws now think these laws discriminate. They would like to see them repealed. Others think the laws must stay to give minorities an equal chance for jobs. Still others believe in the spirit of the laws but think that the term affirmative action now angers people so much that the laws must be reformed.

Think Twice, Speak Once

In recent years we have learned to think twice about the old saying, "Sticks and stones may break my bones, but words will never hurt me." We have come to realize, words are among the most powerful weapons that humans use.

Here is what Atlanta Braves pitcher John Rocker said about riders on the New York City subway and the city itself:

Imagine having to take the [Number] 7 train to the ball-park, looking like you're [riding through] Beirut next to some kid with purple hair next to some queer with AIDS right next to some dude who just got out of jail for the fourth time right next to some twenty-year-old mom with four kids. It's depressing.

The biggest thing I don't like about New York are the foreigners . . . Asians and Koreans and Vietnamese and Indians and Russians and Spanish people and everything up there. How the hell did they get in this country?

—John Rocker, Atlanta Braves pitcher,
as quoted by Jeff Pearlman,
CNN/*Sports Illustrated* Online,
December 23, 1999

As Pearlman says, "John Rocker has opinions, and there's no way to sugarcoat them. They are politically incorrect, to say the least, and he likes to express them."

Political Correctness

Political correctness is a term that has been tossed around a lot in recent years. It is based on a good idea: Using a word that will not offend the people being talked about can pave the way for good communication.

Does John Rocker need a psychologist's help? Is he just a blowhard who thinks any publicity is good for his wallet? Or does he say what he truly thinks without concern for the feelings of teammates and fans?

Words Show How We Think

Words are seldom just talk. They are symbols of the way we think. Words tell the listener what is tucked away in our minds. Our words are a reflection of our likes and biases, and our prejudices.

When we queried Sam Fulwood III as to whether or not he had seen changes in race relations during the past few years, he replied, "Today white people know better, even among other white people, than to call black people 'niggers.' They don't do it. Twenty years ago they were more likely to do it than they are now. And fifty years ago people didn't think there was anything wrong with it. They may not have even been racist people, but that was the way they behaved."

84

Fulwood went on to say, "I think black and white Americans are more tolerant on race questions than they used to be. We see it in schools, we see it in work places, almost every aspect of American life comes closer to being integrated than it was ten, fifteen, twenty, thirty, fifty years ago."

People's words usually show what they think and their actions usually follow their words.

The Downside of Political Correctness

Fulwood also points out that political correctness can hinder communication. We may not want to talk to others because we are afraid we may hurt their feelings.

"Political correctness gets in the way of real understanding in this country. It keeps people from addressing the real issues."
—Sam Fulwood III, telephone interview,
February 6, 2000

Saying what we really think and feel without offending people is not easy.

What's Correct?

Because we don't want to use words that hurt, most of us try to use names and terms that will not upset others. For instance, titles for many jobs have changed to reflect their now being open to both men and women. Examples are flight attendant instead of stewardess and firefighter instead of fireman.

Words used to describe groups of people are often a more sensitive issue. In the United States the term "colored" used to be used to describe people with dark skin of African decent. Then "black," and now "African American" or "people of color" became the acceptable terms to use. Likewise, "Asian American" is now used to describe Americans from China, Vietnam, Philippines, Japan, and Korea.

Unfortunately, groups are not always of a single mind. In years past "Chicano" was used to mean Mexican American and people from other parts of South America were called Spanish and, later, Latin American. The latter term is often still used, as it refers to people from a broad geographical area. Many Latin Americans, however, do not speak a language based on Latin. Despite that, the words Latino and Latina have now become more common. Some feel the terms Latino and Latina are less "Eurocentric" than the term Hispanic, which refers not only to people from South American, Puerto Rico and the Dominican Republic, but also to those from the countries of Spain and Portugal. Of course, those whose families came from Spain do not feel that way.

Confused? You're not alone. The best advice we can give you is to use the term most preferred by the persons in your circle of friends.

But Politically Incorrect Words Don't Seem to Die Out

I was very surprised to see that you allowed the usage of a racial slur in a letter to the editor. Please note that I object to this very strongly.
    —Dick Sakurai, in a letter to the editor,
    Frederick (MD) *News-Post*, Tuesday, July 15, 1997

What was the racial slur which upset Mr. Sakurai? Here is what was written:

. . . when I a kid growing up, FDR, John Wayne, Bugs Bunny, Donald Duck, and others taught us to hate the Japs, Nazis, Italians, and anyone else that might pose a threat to freedom.
—Tom G., letter to the editor,
Frederick (MD) *News-Post*
July 5, 1997

You may think that getting upset, as Mr. Sakurai did, is silly, but as is the case with people in other groups, he has good reasons to dislike such terms. Here is Mr. Sakurai's side of the story.

To explain, he said, we have to look back in time. On December 7, 1941, the United States base at Pearl Harbor in Hawaii was bombed by the Japanese and the United States went to war. Suddenly, the everyday way of life in this country was turned upside down. Food and gas were rationed, which meant that people could get only small amounts. Soldiers were drafted to fight and die on far away battlefields. Right away, many people blamed the Japanese for the changes and hated everything associated with Japan.

Cartoons, comics, and movies during the war years made great use of stereotypes to get people to support the war effort and be against the Japanese. The Japanese were all shown as small, bucktoothed, and savage. They were consistently called "Japs."

As a result, any people who "looked" Japanese, whether they were or not, were also called Japs. Worse yet, many Japanese Americans, although loyal to the United States, were rounded up and put in camps so that the government could monitor their activities just in case they sided with their old homeland.

Mr. Sakurai's family, loyal United States citizens of Japanese ancestry, were put in one of those camps. His father lost his job and the family land. When the Sakurai family finally got out at the end of the war, they had to start over with nothing.

By responding to the letter in the paper, Mr. Sakurai called attention to the hatred implied by the negative term Jap and reminded people that it still hurt him and others like him. By writing his letter and signing his name, he made a brave attempt to discourage discrimination of people of Japanese origin. It was brave because in the United States hate crimes against Asians are on the rise.

Politically Incorrect or Just Plain Silly?

In some instances, the goal not to appear prejudiced seems more important than the goal of not being prejudiced. It makes us wonder if sometimes we are taking political correctness to silly extremes.

Here's a case to ponder: A vanity car tag was owned by a couple whose initials were R. A. P. and J. A. P. Their tag, RAP 'N JAP, was pulled by the state department of motor vehicles, even though the letters were in fact their initials. The department received complaints that the tag spelled out a racial slur.

How far should political correctness go? Did the department of motor vehicles make a wise choice? Or is this a case of political correctness run amok?

Talk Can Hurt

Suppose you are talking with a group of people and someone uses a word for a negative stereotype. Perhaps a man calls a woman "babe" or "bitch." You can speak up and let them know that what they are saying is unacceptable.

Be aware that words hurt. If you know you've said something hurtful, say you are sorry and move on. When you apologize, you turn a long-term hurt into a low-level act that may well be excused.

You may hear members of the African American community use the "N" word. Jews may make jokes about Jews, and gays may use the word queer. But that does not give you the right to use those terms if you don't belong to that group. It is rather like the old idea that you can say anything you want about your own family—but heaven help anyone else who says something bad about them.

Here are some other tips that can help you when you are talking with others:

- Do not make general statements that embrace everyone, such as "Southerners supported slavery" or "I wish I could dance the way blacks do." Very few things in life are true in all cases.

- If someone else makes such a remark, say calmly but firmly that what was said is not always true; for example, "Many Southerners were black."

- Do not say things like, "Yes, he's Middle Eastern, but he plays the violin." The use of the word but implies that it is surprising an Arab is gifted in playing an instrument. Change the "but" to "and."

☞ Use neutral terms such as *firefighter* and *police officer.*

Unless and until we stamp out the subtle prejudices in the everyday words we use, they will be the breeding ground for acts of discrimination.

Writing Wrong

If you spot the use of a negative term in writing or on television, you can also speak up. Recently, a major airline sent a memo to its crews that said in part that they should expect the Hispanics who rode their planes to drink more, carry weapons, etc. When the memo was released to the media, thousands of people called the airline. The public protest worked, and the airline revised its statement.

Writing to Right Wrongs

You can use words to express approval as well as disapproval of issues revolving around discrimination.

Another major airline voted to reach out to gay and lesbian travelers and also adopted policies favorable to gay and lesbian workers. This was a strong move and one that was not popular with many people. Those who took a stand against the airline used the radio and mail to express their feelings. Then, when supporters were asked to voice their approval, thousands (many not gay or lesbian) wrote, faxed, phoned, and e-mailed the airline.

Again, different people had different points of view. Even so, words can send messages to companies and institutions. If people do not support policies of major companies with which they agree, the company may assume that only those who disagree care strongly about the issue.

Can You Judge a
Book by Its Cover?

In his book *Brother Ray*, Ray Charles, the musician, tells about his early life in a school for children who couldn't see. The staff divided the boys and girls into "white" groups and "black" groups. Absurd as it sounds, segregating the children—all of whom were blind—by color was an attempt to be helpful. In the 1940s South, the teachers were preparing the children to live in a world in which people were separated from one another based on the color of their skin. Even if these children could not see the difference between black and white, other people could and would relate to them based on their skin color.

Ray Charles and his schoolmates faced discrimination because of the viewpoint of most white Southerners of those days. To most Southerners, the trait of Ray Charles and his classmates that people noted first was skin color.

Charles's story happened a number of years ago. We still judge people on first impression, but today some people believe that general appearance matters more than any one feature, even skin color.

I have recently worked with a number of poor white women who receive little respect, kindness, or fair treatment. Their hair gives them away, their teeth give them away, their general grooming, the lack of education shown in their speech—all betray them to the police, the judges, the teachers, the storekeepers, as people without power and without a voice. I believe skin color to still be a strong indicator of power and privilege in this country, but not as strong anymore as overall looks.

—from a Unitarian Universalist Association online listserv

Most people make judgments of others based on first glance. You may say, "But judging someone based on one look isn't fair!" You are right, but we all do it.

Those quick judgments based on how we look often trigger a feeling of prejudice that may in turn lead to an act of discrimination.

Many of our feelings about appearance are based on stereotypes. If we label someone because of looks, we then assume other things about the person that fit the stereotype.

Outward Signs

The outward signs we show to others are often the first things that trigger prejudices and acts of discrimination. In truth, there is little we can do about our gender, skin color, and overall body shape.

Other features, such as general appearance, clothes, hair, and body language, we often can change.

Because of that, these features are often even more important than those we cannot change. These features give others a lasting message about how we want to be perceived because they are our personal choices.

Who We Are to the World

Have you ever played a guessing game about who people

are? If you are sitting in a fast-food place, you may look at the people who come and go and guess what their jobs are, if they are married, how old they are, and so on. In many cases you may be right. A woman dressed in a suit with her hair carefully coiffed and briefcase in hand is probably not a grandmother buying lunch for her grand-children before they go to the zoo.

Our outward looks often reflect the real us.

Who We Feel We Are

Our looks also influence how we feel about ourselves and feed into our self-prejudices.

Example: A male, in his twenties, minority, with little education and few funds, who feels he has no chance to make it in a world ruled by whites. He has many reasons for feeling this way. But the result is that he projects, by his overall looks and body language, an impression that will not lead to his getting a job and "making it."

Many of us forecast our own fate and then are not sur-prised when we live up to it. We may blame others and feel we are a victim. The truth is that we contribute a great deal to this self-fulfilling prophecy. A self-fulfilling prophecy can be self-limiting—or it may make us reach high. But it is a very real fact of life for all of us, no mat-ter who we are.

Worse for Women

Emphasis on outward appearance is a prime problem that sets us up for discrimination. Men face this problem but not to the depth or degree that women must deal with it. It affects women of every color in every aspect of life—family, school, social, and work. And it begins early in life.

When I was eight, I was dressed in a lacy frock with a big bow in back. My father told me how he had dreamed of a daughter dressed in ribbons and lace. I wanted my father to love me so I went along with the curls and bows, but I desperately wanted to wear boots and jeans.

—Claudine Wirths

In childhood we often try to be the person our family wants us to be. We also hear stories in which being ugly is equal to being selfish or cruel, like the stepsisters in Cinderella. We may see a mother or older sister who worries about clothes, hair and nails, and frets that people won't like her based on how she looks. From many places we may get a message that "looks = personality."

This equation does not mean the same to everyone. Because the meaning of "looks = personality" depends on someone's point of view, a woman often faces problems throughout her life.

"With a woman, looks are often a no-win situation. In meetings, I've heard people make comments that show they don't want to take the idea of a beautiful woman seriously. Yet they buy into the same idea when it comes from a dowdy woman. At other times a dowdy woman may be ignored."

—Jean Eargle

Being Different Means Looking Alike

After a childhood spent trying to please parents, teens seek ways to appear "different" from the older generation. In their search, they set up situations in which discrimination plays a big part.

All teens discriminate! Young teens discriminate against each other—who is in, who is out. They go on to discriminate on tiny details of clothing, makeup, hairstyle, brand of clothing—you name it!
—Mother who was tired of coughing up extra money for a brand of blue jeans that seemed nearly the same as the pair her daughter hates.

Oddly, the teen group that starts out to be different ends up wearing "uniforms." Gangs and "in" groups are often defined by the uniform look of the members. The desire to be different is a primary cause of prejudice and discriminatory acts against teens.

Young people often style or cut their hair to give them a different look. In the 1970s, many men grew their hair long. Then they shaved it off, wore mohawks, and dyed them with bold colors in the 1980s. In the 1990s, the style changed again. In the next century, teens will no doubt find new ways to style their hair. These styles too will result in biased remarks from some adults.

As young people become adults, they tend to choose dress and hairstyles that conform more to mainstream society, which doesn't mean they will avoid prejudices.

[Reporting a study in which college students reviewed the résumé and photo of job applicants; the only difference was hair color.] The result? As a brunette, the woman was offered a higher salary and rated more capable than she was as a blond, or a redhead . . . The study suggests that societal stereotypes—that blondes are bimbos and redheads temperamental—may make a difference in how a female job-seeker is judged, says lead researcher Diana Kyle.
—*Health,* January/February 1997

Prejudice against someone's clothing and hairstyle is not confined to white women. Shopping in an expensive store? Because of a concern about crime, a group of teens with colorful, spiky hair dressed in ripped jeans and T-shirts are likely to get followed throughout the store or even asked to leave.

The sad truth is that dressing to conform to standards of what is considered appropriate and non-threatening puts others at ease and tends to minimize discrimination.

Diet or Die?

A full-length mirror shows a major feature of how we look, one we may or may not be able to change. In truth, one we may not want to change, if we are healthy and feel good about who we are. But one that may open us to prejudices of all kinds.

Our weight can make us ripe for discrimination, especially if we are female. Women tend to believe that if they do not look like models, they will be rejected both by men and other women. These prejudices are supported by medical advice that says thin is in if we want to live longer, healthier lives. Our doctors' advice gets a boost from an advertising industry that profits from sales of clothes, cosmetics, diet pills, etc.

People who are heavy tend to be discriminated against in some groups, but not in others. In general, a white person who is obese is sized up by other whites and Asians as having weak willpower. On the other hand, many African Americans hold a more tolerant view of weight for both men and women and may even prefer a larger look.

Nevertheless, anyone who is greatly different in terms of size—both height and weight—meets discrimination. Clothes are hard to find. Seats on planes, at sports events, and in theaters are designed for the "average" person. And cars are designed to fit, according to a letter from the Ford Motor company, "an amorphous dummy."

Body Language

No matter how slim or heavy someone is, the way that person stands, sits, and holds his or her body sends a constant stream of messages.

We all respond to body language more quickly than we do to verbal language. If what the person says does not confirm what his or her body language tells us, we believe the person's body language. For example, if someone says "No!" to a sexual advance, but still touches or caresses the other person, it sends the message that the word does not mean what it says.

Body language has strong social meanings. Think about giving someone a high five, an air kiss, a hug. We know each of these shows good will. On the other hand, a sullen look, slumped shoulders, or balled fists send a negative message.

Body language varies with class, culture, and gender. It also differs among groups just as oral language does, so sometimes we read or send the wrong message when we don't mean to. Male baseball players can scratch their crotch, even on television, but you wouldn't catch female tennis players doing it. And if they did, it would not be perceived as normal or even acceptable.

The Stereotype Answer

We are all suckers for stereotypes, no matter how hard we try to see past them. Not only do we use stereotypes to define other people, we use them to define ourselves. We dress like the movie star we admire, or we wear our hair like a member of our favorite rock group. The movies and television and news media bombard us with images that affect our point of view. When we try to be what we are not or we judge people based on what we see on television, we are buying into someone else's prejudices. It does not have to be that way, though.

Ray Charles is an outstanding example of a person who took control of his life and refused to let stereotypes define him. He was born black and poor and became blind by the time he was school age. He refused to be labeled by the physical and social facts of his birth and, later, by the music he sang. For example, at the height of his soul music career he recorded a country music album. All of his life he has been Ray Charles, no more, no less.

Like Ray Charles, you can change a lot about how others view you and how you view yourself. You can also look beyond first impressions to how other people truly are.

Coping

If you're interested in getting a different perspective on your mannerisms, try videotaping yourself. As you watch it, ask yourself these questions: Would you respond favorably to someone who stands, sits, and gestures the way you do? Also use the list below if you wish to limit discrimination toward you that is based on appearance:

➤ Look neat and clean in body, hair, and clothes;

➤ Be proud and accepting of yourself. But consider the response you may get if you wear unusual clothes, makeup, or jewelry to formal occasions, such as a job interview;

➤ Stand erect and walk confidently (or sit erect and gesture confidently if you are seated in a wheelchair);

➤ Refuse gender stereotyping.

Take the Hint

We've talked about the way looks can influence how people view you and how you view yourself. But what if you use looks to encourage discrimination against yourself? No one in his or her right mind would discriminate against himself or herself. Right? Think again.

> Beth looked at her mother as she put on a very short and tight purple and red skirt. "Sure I want to go to Gram's and Gramp's anniversary party, but this is how I want to look." Her mother stomped out of the room. Her older sister said, "Beth, take the hint. A family party is not the place to dress like that."

We all encourage discrimination against ourselves. We do it every day, based on the choices we make in what we say and do. Those choices may not be hard-to-make, life-changing choices. They can be the easy kinds of choices we make as part of life, like what we will wear.

We encourage discrimination against ourselves when we choose to:

↪ Outwardly identify ourselves in a way seen by most people as negative;

↪ Act out a negative stereotype;

⇒ Act in a way that invades the space of others;

⇒ Try to force others to conform to the ideas, attitudes, and actions of our own group.

Encouraging Discrimination by the Way We Identify Ourselves

As young people, you are looking for your own identity. At the same time, you want to look and dress like your friends. But, like Beth, you may trigger discrimination against yourself if you choose the wrong times and places to exhibit how you look and act. If you do so, expect consequences of some type.

Beth may have worn what she wanted to her grandparents' party. Later she may have thought, "Well, the party's over and done and I showed them I can wear what I want." The party is over, but people remember when you go against their values. Sooner or later, how Beth looked may return to haunt her in some way. She may not realize it, but her actions may have hurt her grandparents. They may not treat her with the same respect in the future.

I like to shock people with my black nail polish and my vampire makeup. I like it when they look at me and get upset.
—A fourteen-year-old white female

If you become known as a person who tries to shock others by your looks, you may soon be an object of prejudice and perhaps discrimination at school or on the job.

The results of shocking others may be what you want, or may not be. The choice is yours.

Choosing to Shock People to Make a Point

Sometimes people think that shocking others will make a change in the way other people act or the way people treat them, or even change a law.

Under special conditions, choosing to defy customs or laws may be the right choice. As part of the wave of protest for civil rights in the 1960s and 1970s, many African Americans refused to follow the laws about not eating in restaurants for white people. Many were arrested, but eventually they made their point and the laws were changed.

Before using the tactic of breaking a law to prove your point, confer with others who can give you support and guidance. Breaking a law is usually a last-resort tactic after all other legal means have failed.

Be honest with yourself. Are you going against a law or public standards because you believe in a principle? Or do you simply want to get your own way?

Encouraging Discrimination by Acting Out a Negative Stereotype

Another way to encourage discrimination against yourself is by acting out the negative stereotype. For example, women, according to stereotypes, are not supposed to know anything about repairing cars.

I saw a young woman come out of an auto store. She took a bulb from a bag and started to replace the headlight bulb in her car. Several men came over to 'help' her do it. The young woman smiled at each of the men and declared she would be 'helpless' without them.
— Fifty-year-old white woman

Do you think the "helpful" men would have rushed over to give another man that kind of help?

"But," you say, "by playing out her stereotype, she got help. What's wrong with that?"

When she conformed to the helpless image, she supported the stereotype that women are helpless. Is that the way women want to be seen?

We cannot always avoid acting out our stereotype, nor should we have to, but we can try to avoid the negative side of a stereotype. This is not to say that all women should learn to be auto mechanics. However, women who want to avoid being stereotyped will not brag about being brainless when it comes to things mechanical. A better reply from the woman in front of the store would have been to ask someone to "show me how to do this so I can do it myself next time."

Encouraging Discrimination by Invading the Space of Others

People feel they are entitled to their own space. Anyone who invades the space of other people risks triggering personal discrimination. Space in this sense does not mean only touching someone. It means not entering the imaginary space that each of us feels we live in. This is the space we are talking about when we tell someone to "Get out of my face!" or "Back off!"

Here are some examples how people invade another person's space:

- ➷ Playing a car radio so loudly that the whole neighborhood can hear it.

- ➷ Reading a Bible loudly or praying loudly in a public place.

- ➷ Having a noisy party late at night.

- ➷ Groping, feeling, and more by couples in the halls at school.

- ➷ Cursing or shouting obscene words out of a car window at people walking or riding past.

I recall the night our high school team won the football game against our great rival. All the students joined in a snake dance through the middle of the little town. We sang and screamed and the band played as loud as it could. This went on until three in the morning. It never occurred to us that we might be keeping people awake. We figured everyone in town was as thrilled as we were over the victory.

—Adult white male

When young people invade the space of others, it may be simply because they don't stop to think about how they are affecting others. They do not consider that what they are doing might bother other people. If they and their friends like loud music, rowdy play, or yelling foul words, they often do not stop to think that others do not like it and, in fact, are bothered by it.

For example, have you thought that you may offend others if you talk loudly and crudely in a movie theater? Are you doing it to annoy the people around you? Or because you don't respect their rights? Or just because you like to do it? Is everyone in the theater doing it, or just you and your friends?

If the loud talk is limited to you and your friends, don't be surprised when others react in anger at having their ears invaded. This type of behavior ultimately encourages others to discriminate against you by judging you based on these actions, i.e., all teenagers are loud, rowdy, and disrespectful.

Encouraging Discrimination by Forcing Others to Conform

We encourage discrimination against ourselves even more when we try to force our ways on others.

Suppose you go to a family reunion. All your favorite cousins are there. If you insist on playing loud techno music while the adults are trying to talk, you can count on having the older crowd turn off the power to your amps. You are invading their space and forcing your ways on them, and they will feel prejudice against you.

On the other hand, what if your great-uncle, the one who always talks about how life was when he was a boy, refuses to let you "young folks" play rock music even at a low sound level? He wants music from his youth played. "Try it; you'll like it," he says. He wants you to conform to what he

likes. He is, without meaning to, setting you up to be prejudiced, and perhaps discriminate, against older people.

> *Marta felt strongly about her religion. She joined a
> young people's group that spent Sunday afternoons
> visiting homes and asking people to join their church.*
> *"May we talk to you?" Marta and a friend asked
> when a woman answered the doorbell. When the
> woman found out why they were there, she asked
> them to leave. "I belong to a church," she said.*
> *When they tried to talk to her some more, the
> woman got angry. "This is not how I want to spend
> my afternoon!" When she threatened to call the
> police, Marta and her friend left.*

Coping by Compromise

One of the best ways to cope when you differ with someone is to compromise rather than set yourself up for being
discriminated against. We need to take a firm stand if
important values are involved, but many times compromise is a better choice.

> *Theu's family was planning a big party to welcome
> relatives who had just come to the United States. She
> heard her parents planning the food. They were going
> to serve only native dishes. Theu politely protested.*
> *"How will they ever get to know American foods
> if you serve them what they already know? Besides,
> my American cousins will hate the old food as
> much as I do."*

106

Her parents talked it over and decided to serve traditional foods as well as American foods that would be new to the immigrants, but favorites of the younger crowd.

Compromise is not simply giving in to one side or the other. Rather, it is a way of noting and respecting the value of both points of view. When you compromise, you make room for both points of view to be honored. At its best, compromise is a win-win for all sides.

Compromise is easiest in such matters as food or clothing choices. Note that, at the beginning of this chapter, Beth's mother could have offered her a compromise. She could have said that Beth could wear what she pleased with her friends if she dressed on this occasion to please her grandparents. If Beth had chosen to go along with the compromise, she would not have risked discrimination by what she wore at the party. Compromise is hardest where deeply held values are involved. People will fight when rituals or long-standing customs—those core needs at the very center of one's being—are involved.

Such conflicts can occur in families when parents were raised in different religious faiths. If one parent is Jewish and the other Christian, for example, families may compromise. Or they may celebrate the holidays of both religions. However, if either parent feels strongly that only his or her faith should be celebrated, compromise is out. One person will have to give in to preserve family harmony. If neither parent is willing to give in, family harmony will no doubt be compromised.

Reacting to Acts of Discrimination

When Gloria D. talks to people, her words show no discrimination. She never cuts in front of people in a line. She does her work carefully and on time. She is neat and well groomed. If you think Gloria D. is not likely to be discriminated against, you are wrong.

Gloria D. may well be the target of acts of discrimination that range from low- to high-level if she happens to be a person of color, a person with a severe disability, a lesbian, overweight, or over sixty-five years old.

Discrimination is an equal opportunity pain. Being a nice, good, hardworking person does not protect you. Dr. John Hope Franklin was standing in a hotel lobby, waiting to go into a meeting where he was to be honored for his work as chairperson of President Clinton's human relations group. A white woman came up to him, handed him her coat check, and asked him to get her coat. She simply assumed by his color that he was a bellhop.

What would you have done if you were Dr. Franklin?

Is There a Right Way to Cope?

There is not one right way to cope with every act of discrimination. You have many choices. You must consider many things when you choose your reaction. Some things to keep in mind are: what else is going on, what the reaction of the other person might be, and what that person's intentions were. Keep these factors in mind as we look more closely at some of your choices.

Was It Really an Act of Discrimination?

If you're not sure, it is often better to assume discrimination was not intended. Ask yourself, "What am I reacting to? Is it something I think might not have been meant?"

If you spend a great deal of time getting angry about possible acts of discrimination, consider that there are more productive ways to spend your time. Wendy Kaminer, a professor and counselor at Harvard University, had this to say in the September 1997 issue of *Atlantic Monthly:*

". . . everyone is bound to feel silenced, invisible, or unappreciated at least once in a while . . . An obsession with identity and self-esteem has encouraged students to assume that every insult or slight is motivated by racist, sexist, or heterosexist bias and gravely threatens their well-being. What's lost is a sense of perspective."

Responding to Discrimination

When faced with discrimination, most people want to take some action. If you choose to respond, keep in mind that your reactions can range from subtle to bold. Make sure your actions are thought through, not thoughtless. Some possible responses:

⇝ Turn or walk away from the person or group. This sends a subtle but clear message of your disapproval.

↝ Respond verbally. Deliver your lines firmly without yelling. Say something like:
"That's not true. Here is what is true . . . "
"Why do you say that (feel that way)?"
"Let me tell you why I act (look) that way . . . "

↝ Talk to the person later. Listen to his or her point of view and be clear about your own perception of the event. Consider asking an older adult to observe and possibly mediate such a conversation.

↝ Report the incident to your parents, school staff, police, or groups involved with discrimination cases.

You may find that doing nothing is the best way to cope. Although doing nothing is often harder than doing something, it may be the best approach to take if you feel inaction is in your best interest. For example, if the discrimination takes place at work, with the hope you will quit someday, you may feel that you would rather stay for the time being and then leave when you are ready. Another example is if you may be harmed physically. Your well-being is not worth the risk. In the long run you must make your choice of action or inaction based on what is best for you.

Reacting to a Physically Dangerous Act

If someone tries to hurt you physically, you have more than one problem. If you respond the wrong way, you may commit a crime. If you do not react, you may be hurt or killed. In general, you have the right to protect yourself. But don't do more than that. Think about these steps:

↝ Try to talk the person out of violence.

↝ If it is clear the person will not listen, leave at once. You are not running away. You're being smart.

↝ Do anything you can to get away if the person has a history of angry acts and/or if he or she has been drinking or is on a drug such as cocaine or PCP.

↝ If you are attacked, yell as loudly as you can.

↝ Call the police to come to your aid. Treat the police with respect. Understand that police officers discriminate, too. Do not give them a chance by acting disrespectful toward them.

↝ If you are underage or live with your family, report any incident to your family at once. You may want to talk to a lawyer, too.

↝ Report the incident as soon as you can to the police or to the human relations person at your workplace or school.

↝ If you become the target of a hate group or are not certain of your rights, see a lawyer. Also get all the community help that you can.

Reporting Incidents with a W-5 Paper

If you decide to report the incident to police or your employer or school principal, prepare to defend yourself. Any action you take can lead to revenge by the party or parties who began the action.

To report a mid- or high-level incident of discrimination, first prepare a W-5 paper. A W-5 paper is based on the well-known five Ws: Who, What, Where, When, and Why. Use thinking words—not feeling words. A blank W-5 form and a sample are in the appendix. You will find this report especially useful if, for any reason, you end up in court.

"But I'm Scared!"

Sometimes we do not respond to an act of discrimination because we are scared. Do not feel bad or be hard on yourself. We have all felt scared when it was time to stand up for something. We just did not have the inner or outer resources at the time to do so.

Once in a while you are powerless and cannot respond. When that happens, your goal is survival.

Although all types of discrimination can make you feel powerless, institutional discrimination often makes you feel this sense of powerlessness most strongly.

Cecilia Miguel cannot even tell you how trapped she feels, how isolated, how battered by forces she does not understand . . . Miguel is a minority within a minority, a non-Spanish speaker in a Spanish-speaking portion of an English-speaking metropolis. She speaks only Q'anjob'al, a Mayan tongue of her native Guatemala. The tiny, moon-faced woman sews by day in a garment factory and rides the bus back to her $275-a-month apartment . . . There she cries at night over her three young girls, placed in a foster home because of a bruised eye that she lacked the language skills to explain. "I think about this every minute," a wet-eyed Miguel said through an interpreter,

laying out Polaroids of the smiling girls in her tidy room. "I don't know if they're going to give them back to me or not. Sometimes I think I'm just going to kill myself."
—David Ferrell and Robert Lee Hotz,
Los Angeles Times, Sunday, January 23, 2000

Coping with Your Feelings

No matter what the situation is, you need to cope with your feelings. If you are discriminated against, you may feel annoyed or you may show physical signs of stress, such as a higher heart rate and rapid breathing.

Find what stress busters work for you. Think about exercising, meditating, or playing a game. Many people also find it helpful to turn to a mentor, a person who has "been there and felt that" to help them work through their feelings.

Reacting When Someone Else Is Discriminated Against

If you are neutral in situations of injustice, you have chosen the side of the oppressor.
—Desmond Tutu, Archbishop Emeritus
of South Africa (Anglican)

When we ignore hurtful things others say and do, we are as guilty as if we ourselves carry out the act. If you stand up against acts of discrimination, however, be prepared to become a target also. Before you act, think about what might take place. Expect the person who is the target of discrimination to take the lead. Follow and support. If you cannot help someone who is attacked, run for help. Don't stop to see what happens—get help.

If someone has been discriminated against and comes to you for help:

- ☞ Do not try to convince the person that he or she should not feel that way. He or she does feel that way.

- ☞ Do not dismiss his or her feelings as if they do not matter. That is like telling the person, "You are unimportant."

- ☞ Help the person report mid- and high-level acts to the proper authorities. Help to prepare a W-5 form.

The World Wide Web

Today, many of us also live in the world of cyberspace. You would think exchanges that occur without meeting face-to-face would inspire color blindness and culture blindness. In reality, some see cyberspace as a means through which they can promote prejudice and discrimination.

It doesn't really matter what your religious or political affiliation is, your sex or racial identity, even your taste in popular culture. Somebody out there hates you . . .
—CNET Digital Dispatch, July 18, 1997

All sorts of groups use the Web to spread hate and discrimination. Sadly, a clever person can design Web pages that make the sick words easy to believe, with fun-to-read graphics and gimmicks. But the internet can be used for good as well as evil. You can help discourage discrimination by using your computer. Here are some Web sites for you to check:

- The Electronic Frontier Foundation (http://www.eff.org) defends free speech on the Internet but also wants us to be responsible for what is put out there.

- HateWatch (http://www.hatewatch.org) shows graphics and material from the actual pages of a Web site. Sites are listed if they support violence or hostility toward people or groups because of race, religion, national origin, gender, or lifestyle. Hate sites are listed by the main idea or belief of the group; e.g., anti-Semitic.

More sites are listed in the Where to Go for Help section. What else can you do? If you come across a hate site, you should question what you find. Think about these points as you read:

- Many of the hate sites hide behind a "church" of some kind. They all want readers to feel God is on their side.

- Many of the sites appeal to the concerns we all have about the world we live in, such as money and our way of life. They target the group they hate as the cause of these problems.

- Be careful of links to other sites. Many hate groups hook up with other groups.

- Do not send e-mail to any group you suspect may be involved in violent acts against groups or individuals. You will get on their list.

➥ Finally, *never give your address or phone number to anyone on the Web,* no matter how well you think you have gotten to know them. Meet with someone only in a public place with a friend or parent along.

To get into discussions on a topic like antiracism, join an Internet listserv. You will meet others like yourself who are seeking a broader understanding and knowledge of discrimination and prejudice.

Leveling the Playing Field

I believe strong minds break strong chains.
                              —The Rev. Jesse L. Jackson, Sr,

Did We Come Close to the Goal?

The goal of this book is to help you think about the complex problems of prejudice and discrimination. Hopefully, you will continue to think about these problems. Here are two good reasons to keep thinking:

⮑ Today our country is, more than ever, a blend of people of many different ages, classes, races, religions, ethnic groups, abilities, disabilities, and every other possible defining trait.

⮑ Our life is no longer framed only by the people we see each day. Whether we like it or not, we are a world community linked to each other by television, the Internet, phones, high-speed aircraft, and satellites.

You can ignore the diversity of people in the world and choose to interact only with people in your close and closed circle of family and friends. That's your right. Or you can choose to face the issues we have raised and work to cope with the problems of discrimination.

Activist Jesse Jackson has worked all his adult life to make justice for all happen. In an interview on the PBS show *Charlie Rose* on January 17, 2000, host Charlie Rose asked Jackson if he had done the best he could. Jackson answered, "Maybe not. There were some times when I did not do the best I could . . . But I tried."

Will you choose to try?

Martin Luther King Jr.

The Reverend Dr. Martin Luther King Jr. is best known for his work to provide justice and equality for African Americans. However, he worked hard for tolerance, justice, and equal rights for all people. King called anti-Semitism "immoral and self-destructive." At the time of his death he was advocating for the poor. There is no doubt that he spent his life working for a playing field that is level.

King believed nonviolence was the best way to win rights. His desire to fight for equality for African Americans came from his family, which had long been active in that cause. King was influenced by the teaching of Mohandas Gandhi, who showed the world the effectiveness of nonviolence.

King used nonviolence as a powerful tool. Two hallmark incidents gained national attention. One was the bus boycott that ended blacks having to sit in the back of buses. The second was the march in Washington, D.C., when he made his "I Have a Dream" speech. King's nonviolent tactics of sit-ins and boycotts won justice and rights for African Americans and changed the face of the United States forever.

King was shot on April 4, 1968, at the age of thirty-nine. During his short lifetime he traveled more than six million

118

miles and made over 2,500 speeches for the causes in which he fervently believed. He was arrested about twenty times and assaulted at least four times. His home was bombed and he received a great deal of criticism. Despite all of these obstacles, he never wavered in his work for equal rights for all.

King won the Nobel Peace Prize when he was only thirty-five years old. The Anti-Defamation League of B'nai B'rith says, "His life was truly his message, and today his message continues to transcend race, religion, and time."

Thomas Jefferson

If the phrase had been around 200 years ago, Thomas Jefferson would have been called a great American who worked to level the playing field. You know Thomas Jefferson as the primary author of the Declaration of Independence, in which "all men are created equal" is boldly stated. He was the United State's first vice-president and third President. He worked to make Virginia the first state that allowed total religious freedom. He tried to keep slavery from spreading into the western areas of the United States. Highly esteemed in his own time, he continues to be admired today.

Jefferson also had some flaws that keep him from being a figure we can revere without question. King worked for equality and justice for all, but Jefferson carried out many acts that today we would call high-level acts of discrimination. As high-minded as he was in many ways, he bought, sold, kept, and used slaves. What are we to make of Jefferson's actions?

Despite his undisputed stature in American and world history, for 130 years historians and politicians have dissected and debated Jefferson's views about slavery and racism. By now they are well documented. They were a product of the social class and the racist milieu in which he was raised.

—From a sermon by Wayne B. Arnason,
Unitarian Universalist Minister, March 9, 1997

Depending on our own point of view, we may forgive Jefferson for being a victim of the time in which he lived. Or his actions toward blacks may diminish our perception of him. Whatever our own feelings are about him, we can learn from Jefferson's story: We are all products of our times.

The Reverend Arnason went on to say about Jefferson: "As an individual human being, we can appreciate and sympathize with his struggles, his cowardice, and his courage . . . Jefferson the man still holds up a mirror to me that helps me understand myself."

None of us has a perfect record so far as discrimination is concerned. Each of us has committed, at the very least, low-level acts of discrimination. We need to move past them and look at discrimination in the mirror of what we now know.

Where Do You Go from Here?

Each of us has power. The very fact of being on this earth affects other people. Even if you do nothing, your doing nothing impacts others.

120

Remember John Boyd, the African American farmer who used his personal power to organize other farmers? In January, 1999, the United States Department of Agriculture reached an agreement to pay hundreds of millions of dollars to at least 3,500 black farmers who complained for more than a decade that loans were issued to white farmers but not to them.

Power and Prejudices

Just as we all have power, we also have prejudices. When you hold up the mirror and think about your prejudices, you may decide you want to change some of the prejudices you now hold.

If we truly want to change the divide between people, we must be willing to change the way we think.
—Sam Fulwood III

To change the way we think we must learn more about people. What humans share adds up to more than our differences. William Julius Wilson, author of *The Bridge over the Racial Divide,* says: "There's so much emphasis in our society on racial differences that we lose sight of the fact that we have many things in common—common values, common aspirations, common problems, common goals" (*Charlie Rose* show, January 17, 2000). Although Wilson was referring to race, those attributes are much the same for all people, no matter their nationality, race, sex or sexual preference, age, ethnic group, or ability level.

What We All Have in Common

No one wants to be hurt or rejected by others, to be called names, or to be put down or scorned for birth traits. No one wants to be misunderstood.

Keep in mind these things we all have in common as you think about prejudices you now hold and the power you have to change them, when the facts and your values dictate it.

Some Small Steps

Here are some small steps you can take to discourage discrimination:

- Work to include everyone in everyday, public situations such as school, work, or religious events.

- Think about your memberships in teams, clubs, social groups, etc. Anyone who can meet the requirements should be a member of your group. Do you really want to stay a member of a group that discriminates against others?

- To broaden your own understanding of people who are not like you, read books and talk to people. Think about what you read and see and hear.

- Hold people accountable for what they do and say. If you feel discriminated against in a public place, politely but firmly ask the person to explain their action. If the explanation does not satisfy you, ask to speak to the manager.

122

➣ Be firm in condemning offensive song lyrics, books, magazines, and Web sites that promote hate.

➣ If you have young sisters or brothers, talk with them about treating others who are not like them with respect. Be a role model for them.

➣ Work actively to make the world in general and your piece of the world more inclusive for all people.

Why Discourage Discrimination?

Why should you do things that discourage discrimination? Perhaps the Reverend Martin Luther King Jr. said it best:

"There comes a time when one must take a position that is neither safe, nor politic, nor popular—but one must take it because it is right."

One person can make a difference. That person can be you.

Appendix

Before you report a mid- or high-level act of discrimination, first prepare a W-5 paper. Use thinking words, not feeling words. Write as if you are an onlooker, not the target.

W-5 FORM

1. WHO did the discriminating?

_____

_____

2. WHAT did the person(s) do? Be clear and exact. Describe what led up to the act, what happened, and what followed.

_____

_____

3. WHERE did it happen? Were there others around to see it? Name them and give their phone numbers.

_____

_____

_____

4. WHEN did it happen? Give date, time, and what was going on.

_____

_____

5. WHY did it happen? What, if anything, provoked the act?

_____

_____

If you're discriminated against . . . Only YOU can choose what to do

Act of Discrimination
❑ Low-Level   ❑ Mid-Level   ❑ High-Level

Dealing with the Situation
❑ Walk away; ignore.
❑ Check out your point of view about situation.
❑ Talk to
    ❑ friends
    ❑ family
    ❑ religious leader
    ❑ school staff
    ❑ counselor
    ❑ boss
❑ Talk with person who did the discriminating.
❑ Keep control of your feelings. If you lose self-control, you'll lose.

❑ Using the 5 Ws, write out what happened.

❑ _____
_____
_____

❑ _____
_____
_____

Getting Practical Help
❑ Check library for support materials.
❑ Locate and contact local support groups.
❑ Check on the Internet for information and on-line talk groups.
❑ Take a class to help you cope with the problem.
❑ Report act to group that tracks such acts.
❑ Meet with lawyer.
❑ File police report.
❑ Call local newspaper

❑ _____
_____

❑ _____
_____

Glossary

act of discrimination Any act, minor to major, that expresses biased feelings.

affirmative action Laws that legislate practices to provide equal opportunity for minority groups and women.

ageism An attitude or action that discriminates against a person or group because of their age.

bias A stand based on feelings, without facts; prejudice.

compromise Mutual agreement between people with different opinions or beliefs.

disability Having an area of need so severe that special help is needed to offset the problem.

discriminating Looking at the different qualities of something before making a choice.

discrimination Negative feelings toward a person or group of people; for example, a government, race, or religion.

diversity Differences.

empathy A feeling of understanding and identity with someone else or with a group not like you.

ethnic group A group that shares hereditary or cultural traits.

gender Classifying someone by sex; that is, male or female.

institutional discrimination Acts of discrimination practiced by groups, such as companies, schools, clubs, and organizations.

point of view The personal way someone looks at things.

prejudice   Prejudgment, based on one's own background of values, biases, and opinions.

racism   Belief that one's own race is better than other races: when you act on your belief, it becomes an act of discrimination.

segregate   To separate based on a certain quality or trait, such as color of skin, religion, gender.

sexual harassment   Annoying or tormenting someone with sexual talk or acts.

stereotyping   Belief that everyone in a group shares the same traits.

tolerance   Acceptance of differences among those with different customs, values, lifestyles, traits, or looks.

traits   Features or qualities people have that tend to make them look or act a certain way.

ugly history   Events in the past of which a group (for example, a race or country) is not proud.

values   Ideas and actions that are important to you.

Where to Go for Help

In the United States

American Association of Retired Persons (AARP)
601 E Street, NW
Washington, DC 20049
(800) 424-3410
Web site: http://www.aarp.org

Anti-Defamation League
823 U.N. Plaza
New York, NY 10017
(212) 490-2525
Web site: http://www.adl.org
The Anti-Defamation League, a nonprofit civil rights arm of B'nai B'rith, stands up against anti-Semitism.

Community Cousins
c/o Diane Birnie Bock
140 Encinitas Blvd., Suite 220
Encinitas, CA 92024

(760) 944-CUZZ (2899)
e-mail: biobock@aol.com
Web site: http://www.groupweb.com/cc/cousins.htm

Community United Against Violence (CUAV)
973 Market Street, Suite 500
San Francisco, CA 94103
24-hour CrisisLine: (415) 333-HELP (4357)
Web site: http://www.xq.com/cuav
CUAV is a nonprofit agency aimed at preventing violence directed at gays, lesbians, and others who lead nontraditional lives.

Council on American-Islamic Relations (CAIR)
453 New Jersey Avenue, SE
Washington, DC 20003-4034
(202) 488-8787
e-mail: cair1@ix.netcom.com
Web site: http://www.cair-net.org
CAIR advocates for Muslims in the United States.

National Asian American Telecommunications
    Association (NAATA)
346 Ninth Street, 2nd Floor
San Francisco, CA 94103
(415) 863-0814
Web site: http://www.naatanet.org

National Information Center for Children and
    Youth with Disabilities (NICHCY)
P.O. Box 1492

Washington, DC 20013-1492
(800) 695-0285
email: nichy@aed.org
Web site: http://www.nichcy.org

National Organization for Women (NOW)
1000 16th Street NW, Suite 700
Washington, DC 20036
(202) 331-0066
Web site: http://www.now.org

United States Department of Justice
Violence Against Women Office
810 7th Street, NW
washington, DC 20531
(800) 799-SAFE (7233)
Web site: http://www.ojp.usdoj.gov/vawo

In Canada

Artists Against Racism
Box 54511
Toronto, ON M5M 4N5
(416) 410-5631
email: aar@idirect.com
Web site: http://www.vrx.net/aar
This nonprofit group uses youth idols such as musicians and actors to help teens combat prejudice.

Canadian Ethnocultural Council (CEC)
251 Laurier Avenue West, Suite 1100

Ottawa, ON K1P 5J6
(613) 230-3867
email: cec@web.net
Web site: http://www.ethnocultural.ca

Canadian Race Relations Foundation (CRRF)
4576 Yonge Street, Suite 701
Toronto, ON M2N 6N4
(888) 240-4936 or (416) 952-3500
Web site: http://www.crr.ca
A group that works to combat racism and all forms of
racial discrimination in Canada.

Women's Center, University of Winnipeg
Room OR30
515 Portage Avenue
Winnipeg, MB R313 2E9
(204) 786-9788
Web site: http://www.uwinnipeg.ca/~uwsawc
This center is an important resource for information
concerning women's rights, equality, and
sexual harassment.

Women's Human Rights Resources
Bora Laskin Law Library
University of Toronto
78 Queen's Park
Toronto, ON M5S 2C5
(416) 978-0944
Web site: http://www.law-lib.utoronto.ca/diana

Information about women's international human rights law.

Web Sites

American Civil Liberties Union (ACLU)
Web site: http://www.aclu.org
The ACLU advocates for people whose rights have been violated. The group works to educate the public on a variety of issues affecting individual freedom in the United States.

HateWatch
Web site: http://www.hatewatch.org
HateWatch keeps the most up to date catalog of hate groups that use the Web to recruit and organize.

National Association for the Advancement of
    Colored People (NAACP)
Web site: http://www.naacp.org
The NAACP is the oldest and best-known group that advocates for African Americans.

Southern Poverty Law Center (SPLC)
Web site: http://www.splcenter.org
SPLC works to combat "hate, intolerance, and discrimination through education and litigation."

Unitarian Universalist Association
Web site: http://www.uua.org
The Unitarian Universalists have a long history of work-

ing to make their church "an authentically anti-oppressive, anti-racist, and multicultural faith."

Youth Action for Peace (YAP)
Web site: http://www.yap.org
Youth Action for Peace, founded in 1923, works globally to bring together young people who have as their goal a society of justice, peace, and human solidarity.

For Further Reading

Birdseye, Debbie H., and Tom Birdseye. *Under Our Skin: Kids Talk about Race.* New York: Holiday House, Inc., 1997.

D'Angelo, Laura. *Hate Crimes.* Broomall, PA: Chelsea House Publishers, 1997.

"Disabilities That Qualify Children and Youth for Special Education Services under the Individuals with Disabilities Education Act (IDEA)." Washington, D.C.: National Information Center for Children and Youth with Disabilities (NICHCY), 1995.

Fulwood, III, Sam. *Waking from the Dream: My Life in the Black Middle Class.* New York: Doubleday, 1996.

Garza, Hedda. *African Americans & Jewish Americans: A History of Struggle.* Danbury, CT: Franklin Watts, Inc., 1995.

Weiss, Ann. *The Glass Ceiling.* New York: Twenty-First Century Books, Inc., 1999.

Wirths, Claudine G., and Mary Bowman-Kruhm. *Coping with Confrontations and Encounters with the Police.* New York: Rosen Publishing Group, Inc., 1998.

Index